HEALING WATERS

I will refresh the weary and satisfy the faint. — Jeremiah 31:25

WENDY TORRES, BCBC

KUDU

Healing Waters
by Ms. Wendy Torres, BCBC

Contents

Endorsements

What struck me the most is how lovingly *Healing Waters* is written. Every sentence is a reflection and expression of God's love for us and how gentle and lovingly He interacts with us, even as He is challenging us! Each chapter brings a fresh balm of healing to a hurting, broken heart. Wendy masterfully choreographs a symphony of creative approaches into her healing process, all resulting in the reader experiencing God's love in a very personal way that draws them into deeper intimacy with Him. In an uncertain world where intimacy with the Lord is the only thing that we can depend upon, this heart-transforming book is needed now more than ever!

— Jeanne Nigro
President & Founder of Jeanne Nigro Ministries

Wendy Torres, in her book *Healing Waters,* has creatively designed a unique pathway to freedom in Christ Jesus. Her heart for the hurting is brimming with compassion and a vast depths of encouragement. This unique journal is designed to walk a person out of pain, loss, and abandonment into wholeness, fullness in God, and total acceptance in the Beloved. She in ingenious in her approach, using prophetic acts, personal activation, and an awesome intercessory prayer power. I heartily endorse this book to all who are seeking true freedom in Christ.

— The Rev. Dr. Jack Sheffield
Co-founder and Executive Director of Christ Healing Center

Wendy Torres will not only help you get in touch with your pain, she will take you to the healing presence of Jesus Christ. If you are ready to take action, drink from the cup of *Healing Waters.*

— Sue Detweiler
author, speaker, and pastor.

As I read through Wendy Torres' workbook, it felt like I was sitting in her office explaining my situation to her. Her warmth and compassion for hurting people flows throughout the pages. The Scriptural references are comforting as Wendy helps us realize we are not alone in our struggles.

— Lisa Burkhardt Worley
Award-winning author of three books including
If I Only Had…Wrapping Yourself in God's Truth during Storms of Insecurity

Wendy Torres fuses the power of God's Word, prayer, and her own giftedness and experience in leading others to deep healing, and the result is a compelling, accessible resource. When life hurts, Wendy points you to the God who heals. A powerful tool for anyone who has been bruised and wounded through life's rough ride.

— Jennifer Kennedy Dean
author of the bestselling Live a Praying Life™
and numerous books and Bible studies;
executive director of The Praying Life Foundation

As I read through the pages of *Healing Waters* the tangible presence of God moved upon my heart in a profound way. This 21-day journey offers hope and healing for anyone desiring to be free from the pain of their past. With gentleness and compassion Ms. Wendy guides you though the process of healing and assures you that you're not alone, as she unveils the heart of God towards those who are hurting. *Healing Waters* is not just a book it's an experience! You are sure to be refreshed.

— Kathy R. Green
Intercessor, Author, and Speaker

Dedication

With my deepest gratitude I dedicate this book to My Lord who has turned my tears of sorrow to joy. Father you are my healer, thank you for giving me the grace to write this book. I love you.

To my beautiful children,

Stephen; my precious son, my hope for tomorrow, my first proposal from a 4 year old for marriage, my informer, my first love at first sight.

Elizabeth; my beautiful daughter, my friend, my heart's desire, my constant source of laughter, and my strength in the midst of storms.

Lidia; my lovely daughter, my friend, my reward, my reflection in the mirror who makes me so proud, and my sunshine every day.

Isaac; my beloved son in whom I am well please, my answered prayer, my best snuggle buddy, my hope for the next generation and whisper of my heart as it beats, "I love Isaac."

Joy; my baby in heaven whom I long to embrace, my cheerleader watching from above, and my love waiting for me in eternity.

You are all my legacy here on the earth and I love you with every breath I take now, and the ones I will take in eternity with Jesus. This is for you should you ever need my advice and I'm not here to tell you in person. It's for your children and their children too. Together we will make a BIG impact on the earth!

Finally, for all that have ever hurt me and made this book possible.

I say as Joseph did, "You intended to harm me, but God intended it all for good. He brought me to this position so I could save the lives of many people" (Genesis 50:20).

Introduction

Dear Beloved Child of God, I am so honored to travel with you on this healing journey. As a Christian Counselor I hope to lead you closer to the heart of God, to share Godly wisdom and help you again understanding. It is my prayer that you will be set free from your pain and the torment it brings. As you go through this book, please do so at a pace that works best for you. You may want to do this for twenty one consecutive days or perhaps once a week. You will need a few materials to complete some of the exercises I have planned for you. Before you begin it would be beneficial to you to find a blanket and any pair of gloves you would like to complete some very important exercises.

I am so excited about what God is going to do in your heart and through your life! May this be a journey of a lifetime, and one that restores your soul.

My warmest regards,

Ms. Wendy

DAY #1
Your story matters.

As we begin your healing journey, I want you to write down what you want to work through during this time. I suggest that you process one deep matter or event at a time. I know that many different wounds can occur as a result of an event such as divorce, child abuse, or death (just to name a few), and we will look at the details of the event and examine your hurt over the next few weeks. So, I want you to choose just one event now for this workbook and then feel free to go back and do the workbook again in order to bring healing to other events and pain in your heart. If you try and cover too much at one time, the impact will be smaller, and I know you want to maximize the benefits from your time invested.

WHAT AREA DO YOU WANT TO WORK THROUGH DURING THIS JOURNEY? PLEASE WRITE YOUR ANSWER HERE:

_____

_____

_____

_____

_____

TO BEGIN, I WOULD LIKE TO PRAY FOR YOU. PLEASE FOLLOW ALONG AND ALLOW THE HOLY SPIRIT TO BEGIN THIS NEW HEALING WORK IN YOU:

Father, in Jesus' name, I come into your beautiful presence and ask that you would bring healing during this time that we journey together. I ask oh God, that you would heal this soul, the pain in your child's heart, the memories, and brokenness, and ease their suffering. I pray that you would remove hindrances and obstacles that would try and keep them bound to their pain, and I ask that you release your love and favor now as a shield around them over the next 20 days. Have your way in every area of pain and suffering. I pray that mourning will turn to dancing, and that the sorrows will be turned to joy. Speak to the deepest parts of your child as they journey through this difficult time, and I thank you for being there with them. I pray that you will make them aware of your presence and daily give them the strength to move forward into all of the good plans that you have for them. I ask for these things in the mighty name of Jesus Christ our LORD, amen.

In order for you to heal, I would like you to tell your story just as if you were talking to me. Your story is important. Sharing what happened in your own words and no longer keeping the pain to yourself is important. I want you to share your pain here and allow the pages of this book to hold it for you. I want you to write out what is hurting you, and I ask that you give as many details as possible or that you are comfortable with.

MY STORY:

_____

_____

_____

_____

_____

_____

_____

_____

_____

_____

_____

_____

_____

_____

_____

_____

_____

_____

_____

_____

_____

_____

_____

_____

_____

_____

NOW, LIST FOR ME FIVE WORDS THAT DESCRIBE YOUR PAIN AT THIS MOMENT:

1. _____
2. _____
3. _____
4. _____
5. _____

Thank you. Now acknowledge these feelings before God. Say, "Lord I feel (list the words you just wrote down). Please have mercy on me and heal me." It is safe for you to open your heart to Him and share with Him how you feel. The Lord says that He is near to the brokenhearted, and right now he is near to you. He is not far. He sees right where you are and delights in having the opportunity to draw close to you and comfort you.

HEALING IN ACTION FOR TODAY

Thank you for sharing your story, pain, and feelings with me today. From time to time, as we journey together I will ask you to do something that requires action on your part. I recommend these things because I believe them to be helpful in the healing process.

God wants to be your shelter, a safe place where you can take refuge.

PLEASE PONDER THE FOLLOWING VERSE:

But as for me, how good it is to be near God! I have made the Sovereign LORD my shelter, and I will tell everyone about the wonderful things you do. —Psalm 73:28

IT'S TIME FOR ACTION:

As a way of reminding yourself that God is near and your shelter, will you please gently wrap a blanket of your choice around your shoulders and allow that to tangibly represent His shelter and presence? Allow the blanket to be symbolic of his loving arms wrapped around you and allow yourself to cry, lie down, or express any feelings you may have right now for at least five minutes. Choose during this time to give Him the broken pieces of your heart.

HERE ARE A FEW VERSES I WOULD LIKE YOU TO MEDITATE ON TODAY:

The LORD is close to the brokenhearted; he rescues those whose spirits are crushed.
— Psalms 34:18

God is our refuge and strength, a very present help in times of trouble.
— Psalm 46:1

He who dwells in the shelter of the Most High
will abide in the shadow of the Almighty.
I will say to the Lord, "My refuge and my fortress
my God, in whom I trust." — Psalm 91:1

Give all your worries and cares to God, for he cares about you. — 1 Peter 5:7

MAKE THIS YOUR PERSONAL DECLARATION TODAY AND SAY IT OUT LOUD:

I declare, Lord God Almighty, that you are close to me today, that YOU love me, and that I can trust in what you say. You are my shelter and today I am one step closer to my complete healing. In Jesus' mighty name, amen!

FROM MY HEART TO YOURS

I am so proud of you for opening up your heart today and beginning your healing journey. You are one day closer to a brighter tomorrow. When you need to be reminded that God is near, please grab your blanket, review the verses we looked at today, and recite your declaration. Allow Him to calm your heart and mind as you take shelter under His wing.

DAY #2

God's mercies are new every morning. Loss is painful, and God is aware of your pain.

The steadfast love of the LORD never ceases; his mercies never come to an end; they are new every morning; great is your faithfulness.
— Lamentations 3:22-23

TODAY IS A NEW DAY, and since it is, I want you to know that God has new mercy and grace for you. Sometimes when we think about the future, we can feel overwhelmed by our circumstances and become overwhelmed by the thought of how we're going to make it through today and the days to come. Healing takes place one minute at a time, one hour at a time, and one day at a time. I want you to focus on today and today only. Tomorrow we will consider what that day brings, but for today let's focus on today's healing, today's needs, and today's activities. Moment by moment God's love is going to carry you through today. I encourage you to be mindful that God is close, He loves you, and you can wholly rely on and trust His Word. He will not lie to you and is not to be held to human standards. People will fail us, and sometimes their motives can be impure, but this is NEVER the case with Jehovah God. He is love and all that He does comes from love, and he cannot nor will He EVER contradict His nature. Today He desires that you choose to abide in His love for you. You can choose where you will abide today in your heart and mind. I encourage you to be aware of the presence of God where you're at right now and all throughout the day. He is closer than your very breath, your next heartbeat, and the skin that embodies your soul.

I know that your heart has been hurting, and it's important that we explore the hurt and loss. Can you tell me what you have lost or what has been taken from you? It may be things such as a job, a home, a child, a spouse, a dream, your identity, your joy, your peace, or your purpose, to name a few. Please write out in detail what you have lost.

_____

_____

_____

_____
_____
_____
_____
_____
_____
_____
_____
_____
_____
_____
_____
_____
_____
_____
_____

I am very sorry for your loss. It is okay to grieve over what once was and no longer is. It's healthy to acknowledge your pain and allow yourself to process the emotions.

PLEASE LIST FOR ME WHAT EMOTIONS YOU ARE FEELING RIGHT NOW:

1. _____
2. _____
3. _____
4. _____
5. _____

Thank you for sharing how you are feeling. Now, I want you to pray and tell the Lord exactly what you just wrote down. Spend some time in prayer sharing with God how you feel about what you have lost. Then ask that He fill the empty spaces with Himself.

MY PRAYER FOR YOU TODAY:

Father, thank you that we can come to you with the truth about how we feel. Thank you for listening so intently to your child as they poured out their heart before you. I ask that you would comfort them today and send them reminders of how very close you are to them and how very much you love them. Help them to keep their mind fixed on you, and please heal them from the devastation they are feeling through this loss. In Jesus' precious name I pray, amen.

When we have been hurt and are experiencing loss, deep sorrow, shame, or guilt, it can be hard to believe in God's love, much less calm our minds enough to think about God's love for us. However, you can do this. You can choose what thoughts you want to entertain and what thoughts you want to ignore. It does not change your circumstance or situation; it simply changes the power you give it over your life. The more you fix your mind on something, the more power and influence it will have. When you experienced this loss, God was right there. When you hurt, He hurt with you.

HERE ARE A FEW VERSES I WOULD LIKE YOU TO MEDITATE ON TODAY:

So we have come to know and to believe the love that God has for us. God is love, and whoever abides in love abides in God, and God abides in him. — 1 John 4:16

For as high as the heavens are above the earth, so great is his steadfast love toward those who fear him. — Psalm 103:11

And now, dear brothers and sisters, one final thing. Fix your thoughts on what is true, and honorable, and right, and pure, and lovely, and admirable. Think about things that are excellent and worthy of praise. — Philippians 4:8

"I will ask the Father, and He will give you another Helper, that He may be with you forever." — John 14:16

MAKE THIS YOUR DECLARATION TODAY AND SAY IT OUT LOUD:

When you are consumed with the thoughts of your loss, I want you to choose to shift your focus. Instead of saying or thinking one more day without my _____, I want you to verbally declare, "One more day with my Jesus."

FROM MY HEART TO YOURS

Today I ask you to be mindful that pure, genuine love is your constant companion. The Bible tells us that God is love and that we can't go anywhere to escape His presence. Likewise, the Holy Spirit is always with you and has been given to you to accompany you in this journey called life. The Father knew that you would need a constant companion and He didn't want you to be alone, so He sent you His Spirit. You have experienced loss, but today I pray that you gain a new perspective and embrace the love of God that is with you and His precious Spirit of comfort and truth.

DAY #3

God sees you where you're at.

You have searched me, Lord, and you know me.
You know when I sit and when I rise;
you perceive my thoughts from afar.
You discern my going out and my lying down;
you are familiar with all my ways. — Psalm 139:1-3

WHEREVER YOU MAY BE AT this very minute, God sees you. He knows you and every move you make. He also knows where you have been and the different things you have been exposed to that have made you who you are today. He is familiar and well acquainted with you. Past the things that may be seen of you on the surface, He even knows why you do the things you do. Knowing all these things, He loves you and He likes you! When He looks at you, He doesn't just see you, but He also sees Himself. You have been made in His image, and as your character has been refined, you mirror His one and only beloved Son to Him too.

Though we are surprised at times by the "how's and when's" in life, He never is. Nothing that has happened to you has taken Him by surprise. This being said, we must be careful not to think for a minute that He has enjoyed seeing you suffer in any shape, form, or fashion! When you hurt, He hurts! He longs to heal your wounds and to comfort your spirit today. He loves having you close to Him and having you seek Him for all that you need. Your lifetime here on earth in view of eternity is but a small fragment of time, and the pains you have suffered will pass away. Yet, one day when you pass from this life to the next and see Jesus face to face your sufferings will not compare to the glory you behold.

Precious child of God, have you ever wondered why such hurtful or devastating things have happened to you in light of having such a loving God in your life? Have your tears ever caused you to host doubt and unbelief toward God's loving and good nature? If so, I want you to know that it's normal to do so.

We live in a world that is sinful and occupied by people who do evil. Hurtful and devastating things do happen, even to God's children. However, we must be careful not to interpret hurtful times as meaning that God is not near, that He is not good, or that He has abandoned us. We must guard our hearts and minds and be aware that Satan would love for us to be offended at God because of the sufferings or hurt we have endured. The offense can then lead to separation and resentment. The problem with this is that we can begin to search for a place of belonging and comfort, and in our searching we can turn to the wrong things or people. The further we stray from God, the easier it is to get entangled in sin. All of these things are void of peace and the hope God wants you to have. You have not been abandoned by God, and the truth is that there is not a place we can go to get away from Him. He is everywhere. He is in the highest heaven and even at the bottom of the sea. He is there with you wherever you may be, just as He is here with me.

Jesus said that in this life we would have many troubles, but that we are to be of good cheer because He has overcome the world (John 16:33). It's important to understand that God never promised us a perfect life here on earth. We live on an earth where sin exists, where illness and death are inevitable, where humanity has free will; people choose their words, beliefs, and actions. Without Christ in one's life as the center of their focus and a sincere desire to live for Him, one will live for self. Then one is inclined to indulge in sin and what feels good or right at any given moment. This leads to a lifestyle of selfishness. As we live our days here on earth, we must keep a realistic view of the day and time we live in. We are not in heaven yet; hence, the tears, hurt, sickness, sorrows, and death. The good news though is that Jesus has overcome the world! Have you been disappointed by a less than perfect life event, or life, period? Have you considered that your expectations of a sinless, perfect life are unrealistic and for a time yet to come? The perfect life you desire where you will never hurt or suffer loss is yet to come.

So this pain you have been experiencing is not because God doesn't love you, has left you, or doesn't care. It's because you live in a fallen, sinful world. The Bible teaches us that the wages of sin is death and this death includes, but is not limited to, the death of dreams, marriages, lives, and so much more.

Precious one, I want to encourage you today to look around you and take notice of how God is working on your behalf, of how very near He is. It is important and beneficial that we repent if we have accused Him of leaving us. He loves us way too much for that. His love compelled Him to give up His Son so that those of us who have believed in Him may never be separated for all eternity!

Have you felt abandoned by God? If so, will you tell me and Him about it here and then will you ask God to forgive you for being offended at Him? He is love, and He never changes.

YOU CAN BE HONEST HERE AND ALSO TALK ABOUT WHERE YOU RAN FOR COMFORT ASIDE FROM HIM, IF YOU HAVE.

_____

_____

_____

_____

_____

_____

_____

_____

_____

_____

_____

_____

_____

_____

_____

_____

Now, I encourage you to ask God to reveal Himself to you today and to show you how very near He is!

WRITE DOWN WHAT YOU EXPERIENCED HERE WHEN THE DAY IS DONE.

1. _____
2. _____
3. _____
4. _____
5. _____

HEALING IN ACTION FOR TODAY

Today I would like you to go outside if possible or at least look out your window and look up at the sky and the heavens and contemplate this verse:

For as high as the heavens are above the earth, so great is his love for those who fear him. — Psalm 103:11

If you can, spread a blanket down in a safe place and stare up into the heavens and think about how great, how deep, how wide, and how high His love is for you! Then say out loud, "Thank you Father for such a great love; help me to live in this reality. In Jesus' name."

HERE ARE A FEW SCRIPTURES TO MEDITATE ON TODAY:

For as high as the heavens are above the earth, so great is his love for those who fear him. — Psalm 103:11

And may you have the power to understand, as all God's people should, how wide, how long, how high, and how deep his love is.— Ephesians 3:18

I have told you all this so that you may have peace in me. Here on earth you will have many trials and sorrows. But take heart, because I have overcome the world. — John 16:33

The LORD is close to the brokenhearted;
he rescues those whose spirits are crushed. — Psalm 34:18

For the wages of sin is death, but the free gift of God is eternal life in Christ Jesus our Lord. — Romans 6:23

Where can I go from your Spirit?
Where can I flee from your presence?
If I go up to the heavens, you are there;
if I make my bed in the depths, you are there.
If I rise on the wings of the dawn,
if I settle on the far side of the sea,
even there your hand will guide me,
your right hand will hold me fast. — Psalm 139:7-10

The LORD himself goes before you and will be with you; he will never leave you nor forsake you. Do not be afraid; do not be discouraged. — Deuteronomy 31:8

MAKE THIS YOUR DECLARATION TODAY AND SAY IT OUT LOUD:

I will live, I will laugh, and I will be at peace again in Jesus' name!

MY PRAYER FOR YOU TODAY:

Father, I thank you that you never abandon your children. I honor you as kind and good at all times. Please guard this, your precious child's heart and reveal yourself to them in undeniable ways. Comfort them with your Spirit and help them to make it through this day with more peace and more understanding of your ways. I ask these things in Jesus' beautiful name, amen.

FROM MY HEART TO YOURS

I oftentimes wish that we would never experience sorrows and pains; yet, without them we would not really be able to appreciate the joys and blessings that come as well. I am so sorry that your heart has been hurting, but be encouraged: this too shall pass.

DAY #4
Trust is a choice.

Trust in the LORD with all your heart, and do not lean on your own understanding. In all your ways acknowledge him, and he will make straight your paths. — Proverbs 3:5-6

TRUST IS A CHOICE, AND THIS choice is made by faith. Daily you make decisions to trust, whether you may realize it or not. You have to trust that a chair will hold you up when you sit in it, so you put a certain amount of faith in the chair. Similarly you put faith and trust in stairs when you climb them, not to collapse underneath you. After many times of doing these two things, you have learned that you can generally trust a chair when you sit in it and stairs when you climb on them. The same is true about God's character. He remains the same, and when you need Him, He is there. Time and time again, He listens when you pray and answers when you call on Him. His answers may not have been what you wanted, but He did answer you, and you can be sure that His motive in doing so was pure love, for He Himself is love. Time and again He has provided what you needed, when you needed it. Consistently He goes before you to arrange things in your favor, and you didn't even have to ask. He does this out of His good pleasure and pure love for you.

Have you ever considered the things He does for you without you even asking Him? He keeps the world spinning perfectly in orbit, the oceans abiding in their designated places, the sun and moon perfectly balanced, to provide you with the heat and light you need, and He sustains your every breath and very being. Trees bear fruit for your health and oxygen for your lungs. Choosing to trust Him is essential for obtaining both hope and peace in life. When you trust in His timing, His love, His will, and His Word, it will take a lot of pressure off you that you may be feeling in order to make things happen for yourself.

Have you been trying to find peace and trying to make things happen for yourself apart from God? Has your patience worn thin or your faith grown weary after many prayers have been prayed and many tears shed along your way? Have you been feeling restless about what your next step should be or about how this season in your life will end?

PLEASE SHARE:

_____

_____

_____

_____
_____
_____
_____
_____
_____
_____
_____
_____
_____
_____
_____
_____
_____

Thank you for openly sharing that with me. Trusting in God is a choice and it leads to rest.

PLEASE LIST THE WORDS THAT COME TO MIND WHEN YOU THINK ABOUT TRUST:

1. _____
2. _____
3. _____
4. _____
5. _____

God doesn't expect you to have all the answers for your life, but He does want you to acknowledge Him in all your ways. Take a moment and pray about what you just shared in your writings. I encourage you to ask God to help you trust Him more and more. To see Him for who He really is. To show you what step to take next and to please open doors that you need opened and to close the ones you need closed.

CAN YOU RECOUNT A TIME IN YOUR LIFE WHEN GOD HAS SHOWN YOU HIS TRUSTWORTHINESS? PLEASE DO SO HERE:

_____
_____

_____

_____

_____

_____

_____

HEALING IN ACTION FOR TODAY

If you can, memorize the following and recite it throughout the day. (It may help to write it down in several places where you will see it.)

"I will totally rely upon my Savior's truths."

Totally

Rely

Upon my

Savior's

Truths

HERE ARE A FEW VERSES I WOULD LIKE YOU TO MEDITATE ON TODAY:

Trust in the LORD with all your heart, and do not lean on your own understanding. In all your ways acknowledge him, and he will make straight your paths. — Proverbs 3:5-6

Commit to the LORD whatever you do, and he will establish your plans. — Proverbs 16:3

Trust in the LORD forever, For in GOD the LORD, we have an everlasting Rock. — Isaiah 26:4

Trust in him at all times, you people;
pour out your hearts to him,
for God is our refuge. — Psalm 62:8

But I am like an olive tree flourishing in the house of God;
I trust in God's unfailing love for ever and ever. — Psalm 52:8

MY PRAYER FOR YOU TODAY:

Father you are trustworthy, you are wise, and you are loving and kind. We come into your presence seeking your face and asking for the grace to trust you more. I pray that this your child will grow in their trust for you moment by moment, and day by day. Help them to see with your perspective and to yield to your wisdom. I ask that you would make their steps sure as they trust in you and that you would pour out your favor and blessings upon them today as they acknowledge you in all their ways. In Jesus' name, amen.

FROM MY HEART TO YOURS

The more you practice asking God to guide you and to work on your behalf, the less you will be burdened with regrets for skipping this wise step. You can trust Him; He is faithful even when we are faithless. He loves you and wants for you to rely and depend on Him with all sincerity. He loves it when you come to Him with a childlike faith. When you are trusting Him, you will find your soul at rest. When you are not resting, that means you are not trusting.

DAY #5

Your times are in God's hands.

"For I know what I have planned for you," says the LORD. "I have plans to prosper you, not to harm you. I have plans to give you a future filled with hope." — Jeremiah 29:11

YOUR LIFE AND EVERY DAY you live are in God's hands. He has a very specific plan for your life and a purpose for your existence. Though times have been tough, this does not change who God is and the truth He declares over your life or your future. The truth is that He has a plan for your future, and His plan is to prosper you and to give you a future filled with hope! His plan is for good, not evil, so you have no need to fear. Today, I want to challenge you to choose to believe this truth, not simply because I say so but because Yahweh, your Loving Father, has said so. He is not one to lie, and you can take Him at His word.

Now, I would like to ask you something. Are you concerned about what your future holds? Or do you have a sense as to what God may be calling you to do as you move forward and are unsure as to how or if things are going to work out well for you? Believing that God has a good plan for your future may or may not be challenging; however, yielding to His will may be, if it is not what you thought it would be. I can think of a time when I thought I had everything in life figured out for myself. I thought I knew where I would live, whom I would spend my lifetime with, what my children's education would look like, and exactly how my career would take shape and be carried out. When things didn't happen the way I thought though, I began to wrestle with God and what His will for my family and me was. Things were not happening the way I planned for them to go, and this made me feel as if my world was being turned upside down. In my opinion, sometimes we spend so much time fighting God's will and doubting His goodness that we fail to realize we are unnecessarily forfeiting our peace in the process. We are called to surrender our own will to God's and to live by faith. In exchange we acquire His perfect peace, His blessings and grace for the times we are in. Let us look to Jesus as an example, when He chose not to demand His own will as He prayed in The Garden of Gethsemane, just before He was betrayed by Judas.

"Keep watching and praying that you may not enter into temptation; the spirit is willing, but the flesh is weak." He went away again a second time and prayed, saying, "My Father, if this cannot pass away unless I drink it, Your will be done." — Matthew 26:41-42

29

When you read those verses, do you get the impression that Jesus really would have liked for His circumstances to change? Perhaps He was hoping that He would not have to endure the pain, shame, or suffering. Did you notice that He didn't ask the Father only once? Can you relate? I can.

I want to ask you, have you been fighting God or His will for your life? Are you experiencing peace right now, understanding that though things are not the way you would like them to be, God is in control? Are you living in faith and believing that God's good plan and will are going to unfold in your life just as they should?

PLEASE SHARE YOUR THOUGHTS HERE:

_____

_____

_____

_____

_____

_____

_____

_____

_____

_____

_____

_____

_____

WHAT FEELINGS SURFACE IN YOU WHEN YOU THINK OF THE WORD SURRENDER?

1. _____
2. _____
3. _____
4. _____
5. _____

I want to encourage you to take confidence in God's wisdom and ponder these questions.

Do you know that He knows all the stars in the sky by name? Do you know where the cornerstone of the earth has been laid, or what time He will command the morning sun to rise? Have you ordered the sea to stop at certain places and for the clouds to be wrapped in thick darkness? Have you walked the recesses of the deep or told the darkness where to hide? God knows and has always known and given such commands to the morning and to the oceans deep. Have you seen the storehouses of rain or hail? I would encourage you to read Job chapter 38 if you haven't done so lately. Have you any idea how many hairs are on your head or how many breaths you took this past minute? God knows both! His knowledge is unsearchable and His understanding profound toward life and toward you. Though it may seem that things have escaped Him and His power, this is very far from the truth. Even in hard times He has a plan. Regardless of what has hurt you or how things may have changed for you, He still has a good plan! He is the Master of Redemption and He will take care of you and you will fulfill your destiny! God never slumbers or sleeps, and to Him there is no darkness, so all things are in plain sight for Him.

Choosing to surrender to God's will and to God's love is wise, and it is your faith at work. You don't have to fully understand why things are happening in order to believe that God is taking care of you and that He will work everything out for your good. Choosing to stop contending with Him will bring you more peace. God is all knowing, all powerful, and completely trustworthy.

Please pray about your feelings and struggles with surrender, should there be any.

YOU CAN WRITE THAT PRAYER OUT HERE:

_____

_____

_____

_____

_____

_____

HEALING IN ACTION FOR TODAY

Look up the hymn titled *I Surrender All* and worship with it as you go through the day today. Let your heart, your mouth, and your will worship Him who loves you. He desires for you to yield to Him, to deliver unto Him your pain.

MAKE THIS YOUR PERSONAL DECLARATION TODAY AND SAY IT OUT LOUD:

My Lord's plans toward me are good and not evil, and my future is filled with hope. I will not fear, I will not doubt, and I will not give up.

Keep saying this today until it really gets deep down into your spirit.

HERE ARE A FEW VERSES I WOULD LIKE YOU TO MEDITATE ON TODAY:

"For I know what I have planned for you," says the LORD. "I have plans to prosper you, not to harm you. I have plans to give you a future filled with hope." — *Jeremiah 29:11*

He determines the number of the stars; he gives to all of them their names.— Psalm 147:4

For I am confident of this very thing, that He who began a good work in you will perfect it until the day of Christ Jesus. — Philippians 1:6

Surrender yourself to the LORD, and wait patiently for him. Do not be preoccupied with [an evildoer] who succeeds in his way when he carries out his schemes. — Psalm 37:7

Be anxious for nothing, but in everything by prayer and supplication with thanksgiving let your requests be made known to God. And the peace of God, which surpasses all comprehension, will guard your hearts and your minds in Christ Jesus. — Philippians 4:6-7

Indeed, he who watches over Israel never slumbers or sleeps. — Psalm 121:4

Even the darkness is not dark to You, and the night is as bright as the day. Darkness and light are alike to You. — Psalm 139:12

MY PRAYER FOR YOU TODAY:

Father, your ways are just and your scales fair. I place your child before you now, asking that you would vindicate them and ease their struggles and worries. I ask that they receive your peace that passes all understanding as they choose to surrender their will, their lives, and emotions to you. I pray that you turn their sorrows into dancing, and that you will put a new song in their heart, in Jesus' name!

FROM MY HEART TO YOURS

Your life is precious, and God is crafting and ordaining your steps. At this time you may feel as if things don't make sense; I have felt that way before too. Just because you feel this way though and may not be able to see the future clearly, does not mean that God can't! Of course He can see everything from beginning to end. He is not worried or afraid for one second! His will is going to prevail and so will His mercy and grace. Be at peace, precious one. Be at peace and let go of the idea that your way is the only way and that you have nothing to look forward to!

DAY #6

God is your safe place.

For in the day of trouble he will keep me safe in his dwelling; he will hide me in the shelter of his sacred tent and set me high upon a rock. — Psalm 27:5

WE HAVE TALKED ABOUT JESUS telling us that in life we will experience troubled times. They are inevitable for us all, and they are often used to help us clarify who God is in our lives and to mature us in our prospective walks of faith. Part of your spiritual journey as a Christian is consciously making Him Lord of your life. In your life it is important to define who God is in relation to you. If Yahweh is Lord to you, then you must be willing to follow Him and yield to His instructions, wisdom, and commands. If another person is your god, then you will know by how you live your life in relation to them. You will live according to their words and counsel, and in service to their happiness. If you are your own god and master of your own life, then you will know because your desires and feelings will be your guide. You will do what feels good and right to you as a way of life. Determining whom you will serve, be loyal to, and follow in life is essential for peace and order. Since you are reading this book, I am going to assume that Yahweh is your God and that He is the one you are choosing to live your life for today. Upon contemplation of this though, you may have realized that either you or someone else has been playing that role, has been made first place in your life, and this needs to be addressed. Sometimes the pain we experience in life happens because we have lost focus and have made ourselves or someone else Lord of our life. God says that He does not desire for you to have any other god before Him. This can happen slowly and subtly in life, and it is something to be closely examined. Can this perhaps be true of you? Has someone else or perhaps even you been sitting on the throne of your heart as Lord? Please answer this question: Who has been Lord in your life?

WOULD YOU DEDICATE YOURSELF TO GOD AGAIN HERE AND DECLARE YOUR CHOICE TO CROWN HIM AS YOUR GOD?

_____

_____

_____

_____

_____

_____

_____

Read the following from Psalm 100:3-5:

Know that the LORD Himself is God;
It is He who has made us, and not we ourselves;
We are His people and the sheep of His pasture.
Enter His gates with thanksgiving
And His courts with praise.
Give thanks to Him, bless His name.
For the LORD is good;
His loving kindness is everlasting
And His faithfulness to all generations.

Focus is everything. You can focus on your pain for the next five minutes or you can focus on your Lord and what you find when you enter into His presence. You see, in His presence is fullness of joy, and joy is like a healing ointment for the soul. It doesn't change circumstances, but it does change you. It changes the level of strength you have to stand strong and your ability to endure. The joy of the Lord and being in His presence will strengthen you. Do you know what else is in His presence? Peace is there, because Jesus is seated at His right hand and Jesus is the Prince of Peace. Jesus emanates peace; it is who He is. In His presence is love, for God is love and he exudes it. Healing is in His presence too. Right now, in God's presence, worship is happening, and burdens are lifted when we worship. By the way, do you know that worship is the way into His presence? It is, and the place I long for your mind to be is there.

Oftentimes when we feel as if we are drowning beneath troubled waters, we can become desperate for fresh air, for relief. Come up out of your troubled waters today by entering into His presence, and it will be to you like a long awaited breath of fresh air. I encourage you to look for things to thank God for in your life, and then give Him praise. Thank Him for things great and small, such as, your lungs and your heart. Thank Him for the ability to see and to hear. Thank Him for His love and for how He has been speaking to you lately. Thank Him for your limbs, your mind, and whatever strength is in your body. If you have a job, thank Him. If you have a home, thank Him. If you have eaten today, thank Him. If you have someone who loves you, thank Him. The list could go on and on. I think you catch my drift. The more you thank Him and praise Him, the quicker you are ushered into His presence. A thankful heart will turn into a happy heart in time. I know that as you do this, you will enter into His presence and the joy, peace, love, and strength I talked about earlier will be what you enjoy as you have entered into this hiding place of God's presence. You see, He wants you to have a place to turn to in times of trouble. He wants you to be able to step out of the stress, the confusion, and the pain because He alone knows all too well that there is only so much you can handle. From time to time we all need a safe place to take shelter in, especially while we may be experiencing a tough storm in life. God is so loving and good that He invites us to come before His throne of grace so that we may obtain His mercy and grace in our times of trouble. I want you to know that He desires for you to draw near to Him and to take refuge in His presence from the pains of this world. He enjoys spending time with you.

At times I understand that we may feel as if we do not have an ounce of praise in us, but it is in these times that we should look to King David's example and command our soul to bless the Lord! Most of the time, when we don't feel like praising God or giving Him thanks, that's when we really need to do it the most.

Look at what King David, a man after God's own heart, said. This man was well acquainted with sorrows, pain, abandonment, discouragement, fear, loneliness, and struggle.

Bless the Lord, O my soul,
and all that is within me,
bless his holy name!
Bless the Lord, O my soul,
and forget not all his benefits,
who forgives all your iniquity,
who heals all your diseases,
who redeems your life from the pit,
who crowns you with steadfast love and mercy,
who satisfies you with good
so that your youth is renewed like the eagle's.

The Lord works righteousness
and justice for all who are oppressed.
He made known his ways to Moses,
his acts to the people of Israel.
The Lord is merciful and gracious,
slow to anger and abounding in steadfast love.
He will not always chide,
nor will he keep his anger forever.
He does not deal with us according to our sins,
nor repay us according to our iniquities.
For as high as the heavens are above the earth,
so great is his steadfast love toward those who fear him;
as far as the east is from the west,
so far does he remove our transgressions from us.
As a father shows compassion to his children,

so the Lord shows compassion to those who fear him.
For he knows our frame;
he remembers that we are dust.

As for man, his days are like grass;
he flourishes like a flower of the field;
for the wind passes over it, and it is gone,
and its place knows it no more.
But the steadfast love of the Lord is from everlasting to everlasting
on those who fear him,
and his righteousness to children's children,
to those who keep his covenant
and remember to do his commandments.
The Lord has established his throne in the heavens,
and his kingdom rules over all.

Bless the Lord, O you his angels,
you mighty ones who do his word,
obeying the voice of his word!
Bless the Lord, all his hosts,
his ministers, who do his will!
Bless the Lord, all his works,
in all places of his dominion.
Bless the Lord, O my soul!
— Psalm 103

Let us follow King David's example and command our soul to give thanks and to praise God.

PLEASE DO SO HERE:

_____

_____

_____

_____

_____

_____

_____

_____

_____

_____

_____
_____
_____
_____
_____
_____
_____
_____

I am so proud of you for digging deep and choosing to bless the Lord with your thanksgiving.

NOW LIST FIVE EMOTIONS YOU HAVE AFTER DOING SO:

1. _____

2. _____

3. _____

4. _____

5. _____

HERE ARE A FEW VERSES I WOULD LIKE YOU TO MEDITATE ON TODAY:

The LORD delights in your sacrifice of praise today.

> *But giving thanks is a sacrifice that truly honors me. If you keep to my path, I will reveal to you the salvation of God. — Psalm 50:23*

> *You will make known to me the path of life; In Your presence is fullness of joy; In Your right hand there are pleasures forever. — Psalm 16:11*

> *Then he said to them, "Go, eat of the fat, drink of the sweet, and send portions to him who has nothing prepared; for this day is holy to our Lord. Do not be grieved, for the joy of the LORD is your strength." — Nehemiah 8:10*

> *Let us then approach God's throne of grace with confidence, so that we may receive mercy and find grace to help us in our time of need. — Hebrews 4:16*

It is important that you never underestimate the value of your sacrifice. This sacrifice of thanksgiving that you bring before the Lord is costly, and your Lord recognizes that. When you choose to glorify God and what He has done for you despite the difficult circumstances you are in, despite your desire to complain or speak negatively, you begin to tear down that which seeks to devour you. This, dear one, is a very important and powerful discipline and one that yields a great reward!

MAKE THIS YOUR PERSONAL DECLARATION TODAY AND SAY IT OUT LOUD:

I will praise you now Oh Lord and join in with the angels—"HOLY, HOLY, HOLY is THE LORD GOD, THE ALMIGHTY, WHO WAS AND WHO IS AND WHO IS TO COME" (Rev. 4:8).

My best days are yet to come, in Jesus' mighty name!

MY PRAYER FOR YOU TODAY:

Price of Peace, Almighty God, and giver of life, we bless you today. It's your face and your grace O Lord that we seek. To make you our refuge and fortress for times of trouble. We thank you for providing all that we need now and forevermore. Father I ask for this dear child of yours to be given an extra measure of grace to focus on what is good and lovely and right in their world. Help them as they reach for more of you to remain steadfast. Bless them with your joy as they give you praise and offer up a sacrifice that you are worthy of. I pray that you would consume every word that falls from their lips and renew their hope for tomorrow. May they truly know the power of your love and be completely healed. I thank you for what you have done in them so far Lord and for what you are yet to do. In Jesus' name, amen.

HEALING IN ACTION FOR TODAY

SEE IF YOU CAN REMEMBER WHAT THE ACRONYM FOR TRUST WAS THAT YOU LEARNED ON DAY 4.

T - _____

R - _____

U - _____

S - _____

T - _____

Now, go back and see if you got it right.

DAY #7

A time to rest

Let my soul be at rest again,
for the LORD has been good to me.
— Psalm 116:7

FOR SIX DAYS WE HAVE been working, and now it is time to allow for some rest and reflection. Let's take inventory of the journey thus far. We have discussed what you have experienced, we have processed some of the pain, and we have looked into God's Word for truth so that you could apply it to your life like a healing ointment. You have declared life and victory, spent time in prayer, and challenged yourself to trust in God's ways and in His character. You have crowned Him Lord in your life and commanded your soul to praise Him. You may have cried some too and had beautiful moments as you have opened your heart up to the Lord. These are wonderful things, and I believe you have already begun to experience some relief and definitely some healing.

Rest is going to be our focus today. Let us continue on our journey!

In our pain we can be blinded and overcome by negative thoughts, ideas, and emotions. Our feelings will always follow our thoughts, and when these thoughts are negative, they will lead to negative emotions. When we are hurting, we must exercise our will and strength to focus on more than just our difficult circumstances and pain. This can only happen though if you are intentional with your energy, your thoughts, and your focus. Positive thoughts don't require any more energy from you than negative ones, but one leads to life and an overall sense of wellbeing while the other tends to lead to death and robs you of all joy, hope, and strength. Without balance and the proper perspective of where our thoughts will lead us, we can easily be overcome by depression and anxiety. The truth is that there is more to your life than the difficulty you have experienced. You have to let your mind rest from dwelling on the pain though and choose to focus on God, on His goodness, on His love, on His power, and on His ability to see you through this victoriously so that you can counterbalance the negative thoughts and reflections in your mind! Have you ever considered taking a mini vacation from your troubles for a few hours or for a day? I am writing this book from the Ozark Mountains (which is about seven hours away from home in Dallas, Texas). It is so peaceful here and quiet. As I have been here, the experience has been nice because I don't have the normal demands of life pressing against me. My cell phone is off. The TV is off. So is the music I enjoy listening to; all I can hear are my fingers tapping on this keyboard and the birds singing in the tree. This has been good for my soul in that I get to take a break from the demands of being a single mom of four children, radio show host, and business owner of two businesses. As you can imagine, life for me is very busy. I rarely have time to step away from being a leader and helper to those around me. Since stepping away though I have realized just how hurried I have been living and how consumed I can get with life's everyday demands. Perhaps this may be true for you as well. Perhaps you have been thinking about your pain so much that you have forgotten what it's like to smile or even laugh, and I mean a really good, straight from the belly kind of laugh, one that makes you cry at the same time. Maybe the tears you have shed have stained a once bright and vivacious face. Sometimes the thought of being happy when bad things have happened can make you feel guilty and that guilt is unnecessary. I want to encourage you today to give yourself permission to take a break from your pain. That may sound impossible, but it is worth giving it a good try. You may find yourself pleasantly surprised.

PLEASE TELL ME WHAT IT WOULD LOOK LIKE FOR YOU TO TAKE A BREAK FROM YOUR PAIN FOR AN HOUR OR FOR THE ENTIRE DAY TODAY. DARE/ CHALLENGE YOURSELF TO IMAGINE.

_____
_____
_____
_____
_____
_____
_____
_____
_____
_____
_____
_____
_____
_____
_____
_____

NOW TELL ME WHAT EMOTIONS YOU ARE EXPERIENCING:

1. _____
2. _____
3. _____
4. _____
5. _____

Now, I know that this may be hard, but GO FOR IT! Rest in knowing that God loves you and that He is big enough to handle the burden and pain you have been carrying around. Try for the next hour to change your scenery and/or activity. When the pain tries to come back up and overshadow you, I want you to mentally push it back and say, "No, I'm resting in God right now, and I'm on vacation from you pain!" When you have mastered one hour, then go for two and so on, until the day is done, if possible. Tomorrow we will get back to work!

MAKE THIS YOUR PERSONAL DECLARATION TODAY AND SAY IT OUT LOUD:

I rest in your love God. I rest in your shelter. I rest in your strength. I rest in your truth. You are mighty! You are good! You are trustworthy indeed!

HERE ARE A FEW VERSES I WOULD LIKE YOU TO MEDITATE ON TODAY:

Therefore, since the promise of entering his rest still stands, let us be careful that none of you be found to have fallen short of it. — Hebrews 4:1

For all who have entered into God's rest have rested from their labors, just as God did after creating the world. — Hebrews 4:10

Give all your worries and cares to God, for he cares about you. — 1 Peter 5:7

HEALING IN ACTION FOR TODAY

Please get your blanket out again and gently wrap it around your shoulders. Allow it to tangibly represent His shelter and presence again. Allow the blanket to be symbolic of His loving arms wrapped around you and allow yourself to rest. Out loud, try to express your feelings to your very present God.

PLEASE FILL OUT THE FOLLOWING PERMISSION SLIP AS WELL:

I _____ give myself permission today to rest in God's love and to take a break from my problems, worries, and fears.

Signed on this day: _____.

MY PRAYER FOR YOU TODAY:

Precious LORD, thank you for giving us rest. Thank you for being strong and present in times of trouble. Lord, I ask that you would help this, your precious child, to rest in you, in your provision, in your strength, and in your love today. Grant them your peace and a great sense of security as they look to you for rest today, in Jesus' name.

FROM MY HEART TO YOURS:

Daily we have so much to care for, yet we must pursue balance. We have looked this week at God's strength, wisdom, love, and character. Now apply to your soul the truths you have learned. You are in direct charge of yourself, and you can make a great choice today by allowing yourself to take a break from the pain and to smile or laugh without feeling guilty or ashamed.

DAY #8

He is faithful.

If we confess our sins, he is faithful and just and will forgive us our sins and purify us from all unrighteousness. — 1 John 1:9

JESUS PAID FOR IT ALL. He paid for all your sins when he was nailed to the cross and gave His life over as a sacrifice for you. He knew you would need forgiveness and access to God the Father, and so He made a way for you to have this out of His great love. You see, He has known all along that you were going to commit the sins you have committed. Not one sin has taken Him by surprise. Sometimes you may be taken aback by some of the things you've done, but that is what is so amazing about His forgiveness and His grace; He is not. He knows all things. He is never surprised.

It is important that we reflect from time to time on what the sacrifice of Christ's blood has purchased for us. It has purchased forgiveness, mercy, and righteousness. It has accomplished for us that which we could not do for ourselves because we are sinners. God's holiness cannot be contaminated by sin. A price had to be paid so that we could have access to the Holy One. Jesus' shed blood was holy enough to allow you and me to enter into God's holy presence, to remove our sins and to give us right standing. Again, God has always known that you would need a Savior, so He provided. He also knows that you need His comfort and love right NOW too, and it has been provided as well. Jesus was despised, spat upon, rejected, abandoned, beaten, ridiculed, tormented, and misunderstood by so many. Do you know that because of this, because he too was human and lived here on the earth, He understands and empathizes with what you're going through? Did you know that? He empathizes with YOU! He understands temptation. He can relate.

Hebrews 4:15 says, "For we do not have a high priest who is unable to empathize with our weaknesses, but we have one who has been tempted in every way, just as we are—yet he did not sin."

Jesus became flesh for so many reasons, and one of them was so that He might be able to relate to you.

For a few moments write down how you think Jesus may have felt as he was in the Garden praying, and then when He was tried, persecuted, beaten, and hung on the cross. Did you know that His mom was there watching? How do you think that made Him feel?

45

PLEASE JOURNAL YOUR THOUGHTS HERE:

_____

_____

_____

_____

_____

_____

_____

_____

_____

_____

_____

_____

_____

_____

_____

_____

_____

_____

_____

_____

_____

NOW DESCRIBE HOW YOU FEEL:

1. _____
2. _____
3. _____
4. _____
5. _____

Please take all these things and talk to God about them. Thank Him for empathizing with you and for making a way for you to be close to Him. Thank Jesus for His willing sacrifice. Reflect on the truth that He understands you.

HERE ARE A FEW VERSES I WOULD LIKE YOU TO MEDITATE ON TODAY:

For we do not have a high priest who is unable to empathize with our weaknesses, but we have one who has been tempted in every way, just as we are—yet he did not sin. — Hebrews 4:15

For God made Christ, who never sinned, to be the offering for our sin, so that we could be made right with God through Christ. — 2 Corinthians 5:21

Therefore let us draw near with confidence to the throne of grace, so that we may receive mercy and find grace to help in time of need. — Hebrews 4:16

For the wages of sin is death, but the gift of God is eternal life in Christ Jesus our Lord. — Romans 6:23

(Sin always brings about death of some sort, but Jesus came that we might have life and have it in abundance (see John 10:10). Sin does separate us from God, but Jesus has made a way for us to be made righteous in God's sight.)

For God made Christ, who never sinned, to be the offering for our sin, so that we could be made right with God through Christ. — 2 Corinthians 5:21

MAKE THIS YOUR PERSONAL DECLARATION TODAY:

The Father loves me, Jesus understands me, and the Holy Spirit is by His side.

HEALING IN ACTION FOR TODAY

Faith without works is dead. I would like you to get in front of a mirror, look yourself in the eyes, and sing the song "Jesus loves me." If you do not know it, you can look it up and learn it. It is very simple and very true!

MY PRAYER FOR YOU TODAY:

Lord Jesus thank you for making a way where there seemed to be no way. Thank you for extending mercy and grace to your child now as they have such a need for this today. I know Lord that you have compassion on the weary, and I ask that today not only will your child understand even more how marvelous your sacrifice was, but also how very much you can relate to the pain in their heart. Bring them new comfort today, I ask in Jesus' name.

FROM MY HEART TO YOURS:

Pain hurts and can be crippling I know, but hold on because this too shall pass. If God has allowed it in your life, then He has a purpose for it and not one tear has gone unnoticed by Him or one whispered prayer unheard. He loves you, and one day He will use this for your good and for His glory!

DAY #9
What's mine is mine.

If we say that we have no sin, we are deceiving ourselves and the truth is not in us. If we confess our sins, He is faithful and righteous to forgive us our sins and to cleanse us from all unrighteousness. If we say that we have not sinned, we make Him a liar and His word is not in us. — 1 John 1:8-10

IN YOUR HEALING JOURNEY it is important to take time to reflect on yourself. So today I want you to reflect and take accountability for your words and actions that may be contributing to your pain. Tell me, with the pain that you are going through, did you contribute at all? I think it is important and healthy to take personal responsibility for your actions and words. It is also healing. See, we are not robots with someone holding a remote control pushing buttons that open our mouths and makes words come out. Neither is someone holding a remote control and pushing buttons that move our arms, legs, and bodies, causing them to do things or go places they shouldn't. Our actions and words came from a desire within us, and we will not help ourselves any if we blame our actions or words on someone else. No one opened your mouth for you or put in the words that came out. You did that. No one raised your arm for you, shoved someone, pulled their hair, or kicked them for you either. I understand that people and circumstances can exacerbate us, but ultimately we are still responsible for our own actions and words.

Sometimes it's not even that we said or did something that was hurtful. Rather it is that we didn't say or do something at all, and we should have. We may have neglected to confront a situation or a person and this led to enabling another to hurt us, and this is just as wrong.

Please be mindful that justifying your actions is not considered taking full responsibility. For example, if you say something like, "I wouldn't have called them that if they wouldn't have called me a name first." No, you are not controlled by another. It was your heart, your mind, and your mouth that did it. Wrong is wrong, so don't excuse your behavior.

Thank about that for a few minutes. It's time to eliminate excuses you may have used for poor choices in your speech and in your actions.

After reflecting on your circumstances and pain, is there anything that you need to take ownership of that has not been pleasing to the LORD?

TAKE A MOMENT TO CONFESS THESE WRONGS AND UNLOAD THAT BURDEN ON THE NEXT FEW LINES.(IF THIS DOES NOT APPLY TO YOU, PLEASE MOVE ON TO THE NEXT DAY.)

_____

_____

_____

_____

_____

_____

_____

_____

_____

_____

_____

_____

_____

_____

_____

Thank you for being so honest and humble. Now, let's look at how you're feeling.

TELL ME IN THE LINES BELOW:

1. _____

2. _____

3. _____

4. _____

5. _____

Now confess these things that you have written about today to God and then share with Him how you are feeling.

HERE ARE A FEW VERSES I WOULD LIKE YOU TO MEDITATE ON TODAY:

If we say that we have no sin, we are deceiving ourselves and the truth is not in us. If we confess our sins, He is faithful and righteous to forgive us our sins *and to cleanse us from all unrighteousness. If we say that we have not sinned, we make Him a liar and His word is not in us. — 1 John 1:8-10*

The LORD detests lying lips, but he delights in people who are trustworthy. — Proverbs 12:22

Then if my people who are called by my name will humble themselves and pray and seek my face and turn from their wicked ways, I will hear from heaven and will forgive their sins and restore their land. — 2 Chronicles 7:14

A good man brings good things out of the good stored up in his heart, and an evil man brings evil things out of the evil stored up in his heart. For the mouth speaks what the heart is full of. — Luke 6:45

"Come now, and let us reason together," Says the LORD, "Though your sins are as scarlet, They will be as white as snow; Though they are red like crimson, They will be like wool." — Isaiah 1:18

So now there is no condemnation for those who belong to Christ Jesus. — Romans 8:1

Nothing in all creation is hidden from God's sight. Everything is uncovered and laid bare before the eyes of him to whom we must give account. — Hebrews 4:13

HEALING IN ACTION FOR TODAY

Please take a red marker, pen, crayon, or anything else along that line and go back to where you wrote your confession and write in large capital letters, "FORGIVEN!" The red signifies the blood of God's only begotten Son Jesus Christ and the letters declare your forgiveness.

MAKE THIS YOUR PERSONAL DECLARATION TODAY:

I am forgiven. I have been made whiter than snow through the blood that was shed for me. I receive your forgiveness today Father in Jesus' name.

MY PRAYER FOR YOU TODAY:

Lord, I thank you for the humble heart that you are looking upon today. I pray that your grace, mercy, and forgiveness will be extended to them as you promise in your Word. I ask that your precious will be able to completely receive your forgiveness and no longer dwell and fix their minds on what they have done wrong. Help them to leave these things with you and help them to heal, in Jesus' name.

FROM MY HEART TO YOURS:

When God gives you forgiveness, He doesn't ask for it back. Take this beautiful gift and open it. Receive it with a grateful heart, and don't take it lightly. He wants your guilt and shame to be gone. He wants you to be free of these things once and for all. He does not condemn you. He loves you with a pure and never-ending love.

DAY #10

Have Mercy

Yet I still dare to hope
when I remember this:
The faithful love of the Lord never ends!
His mercies never cease.
Great is his faithfulness;
his mercies begin afresh each morning.
I say to myself, "The Lord is my inheritance;
therefore, I will hope in him!"
The Lord is good to those who depend on him,
to those who search for him.
So it is good to wait quietly
for salvation from the Lord. — Lamentations 3:21-26

MERCY, GRACE, AND FORGIVENESS are yours for the taking. Will you accept them? Or will you turn and walk away? As each new day dawns, God has new mercy and grace to see you though that day. So when you awakened this morning, you had a free gift waiting for you that you didn't have yesterday! You may wonder sometimes how you are going to make it through the next few weeks, months, or even years. The answer is by taking it one day at a time and utilizing the fresh mercy and grace that God has for you on a daily basis. Tomorrow may look unbearable; you do not have the mercy and grace to face that day yet. You can trust in His faithfulness to meet your needs on a daily basis. Be careful not to get ahead of yourself, but allow God to show you His faithfulness day by day. The very things your soul needs with each second, minute, hour, day, week, month, and year has been provided for you and it's free to you if you want it.

I would like you to just sit a moment with that thought, understanding that you are in need of His mercy and grace and that every day He freely gives you what you need in your life to make it through. He is not asking you to live any day of your life alone, without hope or without His provision. He is also not asking you to live out the next five years of your life today.

Take at least five minutes to reflect.

Do you think that God needs help being God? I don't think so. He never sought counsel from a people in how to be God. No one told him how to create man, woman, seas, trees, animals, oceans, or galaxies. He alone is all knowing and full of wisdom. He is always truthful, and this never changes. This being so, I encourage you to reflect on another truth. Reflect and ponder this: YOU HAVE BEEN FORGIVEN BY GOD FOR THE SINS YOU HAVE COMMITTED. I know that we looked at this previously, but I want to take it one step further.

Today, will you choose to not only accept His forgiveness but to also forgive yourself? See, oftentimes we hold resentment toward ourselves, and we don't even realize it. The sense of shame and regret that you may be carrying around is not coming from your loving Father. The expectations we can have on ourselves can be rather harsh and unrealistic! See, though you may have known better than to carry out whatever part you played in this pain, you're not perfect. The truth is that you will never be as long as you live here on this earth. You were born with a sinful nature, and sometimes that flesh does get the best of us. Today is the day though, the day to say, "I am forgiven by God, and today I forgive myself." The reality is that what's done is in fact DONE! You can't change it. You can't wish it away. You can't eat it away, smoke it away, drink it away, work it away, or anything of the like. God is bigger than your mistake though, and He can take that very thing that you regret and ponder over and over again in your mind and use it for your good. He specializes in this. Let's look at Romans 8:28. "And we know that God works ALL things together for the good of those that love Him and called according to His purpose." Wouldn't it be nice to live without that guilt and shame anymore? Not guilt and shame from God, because you know He has forgiven you, but guilt and shame for yourself? Wouldn't it be nice to be free, once and for all? That reality is one simple decision away. It can be obtained in your very next breath if you like. Simply choose to forgive yourself. Today I hope you choose not to punish yourself any longer. Enough is enough! Are you ready? Jesus has already borne your shame, and He has made your sins, though they be as red as scarlet, as white as snow. By faith go ahead now and not only let your regret, your shame, and your guilt be cleansed by the blood of the Lamb, let it be forgotten by you. You can do this.

Have you ever considered that you may not have forgiven yourself for how you may have contributed to the hurt you are working though?

PLEASE WRITE YOUR THOUGHTS DOWN HERE:

_____

_____

_____

_____

_____

_____

_____

_____

_____

NOW, LIST WAYS THAT YOU HAVE BEEN HARD ON YOURSELF:

1._____
2._____
3._____
4._____
5._____

God daily extends new mercy to you. Will you extend mercy to yourself?

WRITE OUT A PRAYER HERE AND ASK GOD TO HELP YOU EXTEND HIS GIFTS OF MERCY, GRACE, AND FORGIVENESS TO YOURSELF. IT IS TIME TO LOOSE YOURSELF FROM THE CHAINS THAT HAVE KEPT YOU BOUND HERE!

_____
_____
_____
_____
_____
_____

HOW CAN YOU SHOW YOURSELF MERCY AND FORGIVENESS ON A DAILY BASIS?

1._____
2._____
3._____
4._____
5._____

A FEW OF MY IDEAS ARE THESE:

1. Do not speak poorly or meanly about yourself.

2. Do not call yourself negative names like "stupid."

3. Stop rehearsing your wrongs in your mind.

4. Positively affirm yourself out loud.

5. Don't judge your poor actions or words from the days before by the understanding and growth you have now.

HERE ARE A FEW VERSES FOR YOU TO MEDITATE ON TODAY:

Therefore do not worry about tomorrow, for tomorrow will worry about itself. Each day has enough trouble of its own. — Matthew 6:34

As far as the east is from the west, So far has He removed our transgressions from us. Just as a father has compassion on his children, So the LORD has compassion on those who fear Him. For He Himself knows our frame; He is mindful that we are but dust. As for man, his days are like grass; As a flower of the field, so he flourishes. — Psalm 103:12-15

But he was pierced for our transgressions, he was crushed for our iniquities; the punishment that brought us peace was on him, and by his wounds we are healed. — Isaiah 53:5

For judgment is without mercy to one who has shown no mercy. Mercy triumphs over judgment. — James 2:13

But like the Holy One who called you, be holy yourselves also in all your behavior; because it is written, "YOU SHALL BE HOLY, FOR I AM HOLY."
— 1 Peter 1:15-16

Isn't it wonderful to belong to and serve such a wonderful and loving God? Today will you thank Him for being so loving and for revealing His truths to you?

WILL YOU ALSO WRITE A LETTER OF FORGIVENESS TO YOURSELF?

_____
_____
_____
_____
_____
_____
_____
_____
_____

_____
_____
_____
_____
_____
_____
_____
_____
_____
_____
_____
_____
_____
_____
_____
_____
_____
_____
_____

NOW, DESCRIBE HOW YOU'RE FEELING:

1. _____
2. _____
3. _____
4. _____
5. _____

MAKE THIS YOUR DECLARATION TODAY AND SAY IT OUT LOUD:

I choose to forgive myself. I accept who I am as God's beloved. Moving forward, I will also quit beating myself up. I am forgiven, I am merciful, and I am kind!

MY PRAYER FOR YOU TODAY:

Lord God of all the earth and all that it contains, blessed be your name forevermore. I ask that today you will uphold your child with your righteous right hand and help them to embrace themselves, forgive themselves, and extend mercy to themselves as you have done for them. Help them to learn from you. I pray that they will learn from their mistakes and that you will give them the grace to overcome the temptation to err the same way away. I thank you that every day you have new mercy and grace for them, and I ask that you would help them to release their failures unto the foot of the cross and leave them there, in Jesus' precious name, amen.

FROM MY HEART TO YOURS:

I am so thankful that we don't have to be perfect in order for God to love us! Remember that Jesus paid it all and His blood is enough to cover your sins for all times! It is also enough to make you acceptable in His presence for all times. Sometimes we don't realize that we are not allowing ourselves to enjoy life today because we are walking around with tremendous amounts of shame and regret. And we ourselves can let those go. I hope that today you are wearing a big smile after choosing to forgive yourself. It is important to learn from your mistakes, but do not be your own worst enemy. It's time to really walk in your freedom. Jesus paid a great price for it!

DAY #11
It's time to commit.

Commit your way to the Lord;
trust in him and he will do this:
He will make your righteous reward shine like the dawn,
your vindication like the noonday sun. — Psalm 37:5-6

YOU ARE IN GOD'S HANDS and you are safe there. His hands are powerful; they are strong, and they intend you no harm. These hands have the power to heal and the power to chastise, the power to set captives free and to bind up the brokenhearted.

Have other hands possibly hurt you in this painful event you are working through? Do you know where this person(s) who hurt you is right now? Or has this person hurt you in other ways that did not involve violence? Either way it's important in your healing process to recognize that you don't need to hold onto their hurtful ways in your heart anymore. They belong to God and so does your vindication! God does not desire that you hold onto this pain. Into His hands He wants for you to commit both the pain and the person(s) involved.

Today I want you to work on committing them to the Lord. I want you to intentionally bring them before your Father in heaven. I'm not asking for you to do much more than that. This entire situation belongs to Him, and it's time to commit unto God those who have hurt you. The benefit of bringing them before the Lord is that you are able to recognize that you are not alone and that God has His hands on this person. You don't need to hold them; it's time to place them in the hands they belong in. His hands are holy; they are righteous tools, and He can be trusted to do what is right at the right time with everyone involved.

Let us take some time now of commitment where you will bring this person or people before God and say Lord here is _____. I have been hurt so badly by them, and I place them in your hands. You don't need to tell Him what to do with them. He doesn't need help being God.

OKAY, NOW WRITE THAT OUT:

_____

_____

_____

_____

_____

_____

_____

_____

_____

_____

_____

_____

_____

_____

_____

SHARE YOUR FEELINGS WITH ME HERE BY DESCRIBING THEM IN FIVE WORDS:

1. _____

2. _____

3. _____

4. _____

5. _____

Now turn those emotions you just expressed into a prayer and share them with the Father. I encourage you to leave those in God's throne room.

MAKE THIS YOUR PERSONAL DECLARATION TODAY AND SAY IT OUT LOUD:

My God is mighty and He is working mightily on my behalf. The Lord is my helper, and I will not fear. I am an overcomer, and my best days are still ahead of me. In Jesus' name.

HERE ARE A FEW VERSES I WOULD LIKE YOU TO MEDITATE ON TODAY:

A Psalm of David.
Do not fret because of evildoers,
Be not envious toward wrongdoers.
For they will wither quickly like the grass
And fade like the green herb. — Psalm 37:7

Be still before the LORD and wait patiently for him;
do not fret when people succeed in their ways,
when they carry out their wicked schemes.
Commit your way to the Lord;
trust in him and he will do this:
He will make your righteous reward shine like the dawn,
your vindication like the noonday sun. — Psalm 37:5-6

In his hand is the life of every creature and the breath of all mankind. — Job 12:10

So I reflected on all this and concluded that the righteous and the wise and what they do are in God's hands, but no one knows whether love or hate awaits them. — Ecclesiastes 9:1

My sheep listen to my voice; I know them, and they follow me. I give them eternal life, and they shall never perish; no one will snatch them out of my hand. My Father, who has given them to me, is greater than all; no one can snatch them out of my Father's hand. I and the Father are one. — John 10:27-30

HEALING IN ACTION FOR TODAY

Today you will need a pair of gloves or oven mitts, a small piece of paper, and something to write with. Now, get the piece of paper and write down the name(s) of the person(s) who hurt you. Then get the pair of gloves and hold them in your lap for a second. I know that these are just ordinary gloves, but today I would like you to allow them to represent the hands of Jesus to you. I would like you to place your hands in the gloves now and imagine as if you are holding hands with Jesus. Oftentimes when we gather with people or pray for them, we hold hands, and this is just symbolic of that. Now, think about this scripture: My sheep listen to my voice; I know them, and they follow me. I give them eternal life, and they shall never perish; no one will snatch them out of my hand. My Father, who has given them to me, is greater than all; no one can snatch them out of my Father's hand. I and the Father are one" (John 10:27-30). As you hold His hands, share with Him what's in your heart and then sit quietly for a moment and allow the Holy Spirit to minister to you. When you are finished, take your hands out and place the piece of paper that has the name(s) of the one(s) who hurt you in the gloves and place the gloves aside.

MY PRAYER FOR YOU TODAY:

Precious God, I love you. I thank you that you see all things and that your power is at work in this your precious child's life today. Grant them the strength to bring their offender before you and to leave them with you. We recognize that you are God, you are mighty, and that you don't need our help in being God of _____ (offender's name). We do seek your grace and your wisdom for this day though and commit to you every broken piece of your child's heart, in Jesus' name.

FROM MY HEART TO YOURS:

God knows how much you have been hurting, and he cares about what you're feeling right now. Bringing your offender to Him will give you inner strength and help you to develop godly character. I trust that you will be able to leave them there and commit them, who they are, and what they have done into God's hands and walk away knowing that God is watching over every detail concerning you and them. I believe in you and your desire to move out of this place of pain and into a new place of love and freedom! Day by day, you keep getting stronger and freer, and this is exactly the way God desires for you to live. I can only imagine how proud our Father in Heaven is as He watches you hand this person(s) over and trust Him with them.

DAY #12

Let us be peacemakers.

God blesses those who work for peace, for they will be called the children of God. — Matthew 5:9

Precious child of God, you are called to be a peacemaker. It's important here to clarify between peacemaker and peace*keeper*. There is a difference. A peacemaker does what it takes to be at peace with another, which usually requires a confrontation of sorts and sometimes an apology. A peacekeeper will avoid talking about issues divisive to a relationship and pretend nothing is wrong or nothing has happened. There is no real peace in that; rather, there is a sense of tension, even if it is not acknowledged out loud. God wants you to be ruled by peace and to have peace as a measuring tool in life. God says that He leads His children forth in peace; this is a way you can know you are in His will. When peace is absent from a decision, you should probably not make another move in that direction. Change your route and the Holy Spirit within you will bear witness to your soul by giving you peace. This peace is not forced, and sometimes it does not make sense, but it is a way that God speaks to us.

Now that we have worked to get things cleared up between you and God and you and yourself, let's move on. When we sin in life, we first sin against God and His righteousness, and then against ourselves and others. Today we are going to work on anything that needs to be confessed between you and someone else for the purpose of pursing peace. I understand that once we have worked through confession and received forgiveness, oftentimes an unsettled feeling still exists because we have not made peace with the one(s) we have wronged or hurt. Today I want to help you unload this burden even more and work through the process of an apology where it may be needed.

The following exercise is for your benefit, and if you choose to send it to anyone, that is between you and the Lord. My purpose in the exercise is not for that. This is for your benefit and to help you continue to gain victory in your life. At the appointed time, it may be appropriate to share these words, and I think it's good for you to be prepared. I understand that this is not always possible, and if this is not possible, I still wish for you to complete the exercise just as if you could communicate with the one you hurt. Now, understanding that we alone are responsible for our behaviors and words, it is important that we take ownership of our words and actions without justifying our behavior to others or excusing them.

I want you to write a letter, as if you were going to give it to the one you wronged, and take responsibility for your words, actions, and intents. Only you can own your behavior, and it's time to do so as if you were talking with the one you wronged. This is not a time to focus on what they did to you—we will get to that—but this a time for you to focus on the pain you may have caused them. Remember, these things have been forgiven by your loving Father and by yourself, but it is important that you have the opportunity to express yourself to anyone you have hurt as well. If you do not believe this applies to you, then please move on to the next day.

Please write your letter here. Remember, this is not a letter where you are to justify or excuse yourself, but to fully own what your part was in this, if any at all. Also consider how you may have made them feel and fully acknowledge that. Use the words, "I was wrong when I …" and then continue.

_____

_____

_____

_____

_____

_____

_____

_____

_____

_____

_____

_____

_____

_____

_____

_____

_____

_____

_____

_____

_____

_____

NOW, TELL ME HOW YOU'RE FEELING USING FIVE WORDS:

1. _____

2. _____

3. _____

4. _____

5. _____

Jesus wants your burdens to be easy and your yolk to be light, and I trust that this has just lightened your load. If you wish to share your thoughts and feelings in the above exercise with the one you wronged, I ask that you complete this workbook first, and then prayerfully consider reaching out to those you may have wronged. They may or may not want to hear from you, but either way is okay. This day's exercise is designed to help you release what you would like to share if given the opportunity.

MAKE THIS YOUR PERSONAL DECLARATION TODAY:

I am a peacemaker. I am God's beloved child. I am getting stronger every day, and I know Jesus loves me! I am precious in God's eyes, and His love is never-ending. I receive the grace of God on my life to be a peacemaker.

HERE ARE A FEW VERSES I WOULD LIKE YOU TO MEDITATE ON TODAY:

God blesses those who work for peace, for they will be called the children of God. — Matthew 5:9

So will My word be which goes forth from My mouth; It will not return to Me empty, Without accomplishing what I desire, And without succeeding in the matter for which I sent it. For you will go out with joy And be led forth with peace; The mountains and the hills will break forth into shouts of joy before you, And all the trees of the field will clap their hands. — Isaiah 55:11-12

Make every effort to live in peace with everyone and to be holy; without holiness no one will see the Lord. — Hebrews 12:14

But He gives a greater grace. Therefore it says, "GOD IS OPPOSED TO THE PROUD, BUT GIVES GRACE TO THE HUMBLE." — James 4:6

So if the Son sets you free, you will be free indeed. — John 8:36

For my yoke is easy and my burden is light. — Matthew 11:30

But I say to you that everyone who is angry with his brother shall be guilty before the court; and whoever says to his brother, "You good-for-nothing," shall be guilty before the supreme court; and whoever says, "You fool," shall be guilty enough to go into the fiery hell. Therefore if you are presenting your offering at the altar, and there remember that your brother has something against you, leave your offering there before the altar and go; first be reconciled to your brother, and then come and present your offering. — Matthew 5:22-24

Dear brothers and sisters, I close my letter with these last words: Be joyful. Grow to maturity. Encourage each other. Live in harmony and peace. Then the God of love and peace will be with you. — 2 Corinthians 13:11

MY PRAYER FOR YOU TODAY:

Father of love and peace, I bring your child before you asking that you would cover them in both your love and peace today. I ask Father that you will lighten their load and help them to release the burden they have been carrying about their own behavior even more than before. I pray that joy will begin to break forth in their hearts. I ask for your perfect timing in approaching the ones they have wronged if they should do so. Grant them the peace that passes all understanding and the courage to obey your holy Word. Lift them up as they humble themselves under your mighty and holy hand. Place them where they need to be today and order their every step. I pray that you would grace them with unexpected blessings and tangible favor. I place them before your throne again oh God for the comfort and strength that only you can give in Jesus' holy name, amen.

FROM MY HEART TO YOURS:

Today I want to encourage you to NEVER forfeit your peace! Our loving and gracious God has given it to you to help guide you along on your path in life. If you feel uneasy about something you are doing or a decision you need to make, then stop. Pause as long as necessary until you have a clearer direction and obtain peace. This will usually help you eliminate many regrets in life as well, and that is an excellent way to live!

I don't know if you can or ever will be able to approach the one(s) you have wronged, but I do know that if it is possible and you have a peace about it, then you should. Making right your wrongs is not only commendable, but it is an act of worship to God as you humble yourself before Him and another. As you humble yourself, He watches you and according to His promise and Word, He will lift you up! The other person may not care to hear what you have to say, and that is okay; your obedience to God does not need to be based upon someone else's approval. God says He refuses the proud and gives grace to the humble and by humbling yourself, you are lining yourself up to receive more and more grace for your daily living. Do this not only for the ones you have wronged, but do it for yourself as well! I. AM. SO. PROUD. OF. YOU!

DAY #13

Forgiveness and trust are two totally different things.

Trust in the LORD with all your heart
And do not lean on your own understanding.
In all your ways acknowledge Him,
And He will make your paths straight. — Proverbs 3:5-6

UNDERSTANDING THAT THERE IS A difference between forgiveness and trust is essential. Forgiveness and trust are two very different things, and I want you to be careful not to confuse them or assume that one means the same as the other. If you give forgiveness, that does not mean that you need to give trust to the one who has done you wrong as well. In 1 Corinthians 4:2, we are instructed that before we are to trust someone, they are to show themselves trustworthy and/or faithful to us. Oftentimes people think that if they forgive someone, then that means they automatically have to trust them or be in a relationship with them again, and this is NOT so. Giving forgiveness simply means that you are taking yourself off the throne as judge and letting God handle your matter for you. You are canceling the debt they owe you and turning to God for the recompense and healing your soul needs and longs for. You are also making a willful choice not to demand repayment from them. Consider these points:

- We are told to forgive in the Bible, but we are not told we have to trust our offender.

- Wisdom would say that trust should be regained after a period of time in which the offender is repentant. When they consistently show that they are being truthful, trustworthy, and have changed. This will help you gain confidence in them at a gradual and progressive pace.

- There is a difference between someone being repentant and someone who feels remorseful. Feeling remorseful (or sorry) for a wrong committed is the right and proper emotion. This does not mean that the person is repentant, and has or is willing to do whatever it takes to change. Oftentimes unhealthy behavior patterns remain in place because remorse is confused for repentance. Remorse has more to do with the feelings involved with wrongs committed, and repentance has to do with a change in behaviors that were wrong.

Have you possibly mistaken forgiveness and trust for meaning the same thing?

PLEASE EXPRESS YOUR THOUGHTS ABOUT THIS HERE:

_____
_____
_____
_____
_____
_____

WHEN IT COMES TO YOUR OFFENDER, HAVE YOU SEEN REMORSE OR REPENTANCE? EXPLAIN.

_____
_____
_____
_____
_____
_____

Understanding that there is a difference between forgiveness and trust, are there any actions you need to consider? If you wish to remain in a relationship with someone who has seriously hurt you, please list a few things you need to see different about them as you move forward.

CONSIDER SMALL AND GRADUAL STEPS AS WELL AS MILESTONES, MIXED WITH A TIMELINE.

_____
_____
_____
_____
_____
_____

HERE ARE A FEW VERSES I WOULD LIKE YOU TO MEDITATE ON TODAY:

Now it is required that those who have been given a trust must prove faithful.
— _1 Corinthians 4:2_

It is better to take refuge in the LORD than to trust in humans. — Psalm 118:8

This is what the LORD says: "Cursed is the one who trusts in man, who draws strength from mere flesh and whose heart turns away from the LORD." — Jeremiah 17:5

And be you kind one to another, tenderhearted, forgiving one another, even as God for Christ's sake has forgiven you. — Ephesians 4:32

Forbearing one another, and forgiving one another, if any man have a quarrel against any: even as Christ forgave you, so also do you. — Colossians 3:13

MY PRAYER FOR YOU TODAY:

Dear Lord of all heaven and earth, I bless your holy name. You alone are wise and good, and there is none like you. You are faithful, you are truth, and you are a God of both mercy and justice. I pray for this your beloved child, and ask that you would help them to gain understanding and discernment about the difference between forgiveness and trust. Please keep them from any false sense of shame and guilt. Help them to walk in the light of your love and to be set free from lies they may have believed about forgiveness meaning trusting those who have hurt them. Help them to see their situation through your eyes. I pray in the holy name of Jesus.

MAKE THIS YOUR PERSONAL DECLARATION FOR TODAY:

I have the mind of Christ. The Spirit of the Living God abides in me. I can do all things through Christ who gives me strength.

FROM MY HEART TO YOURS:

I believe that wherever you are right now that God is there with you. I believe that He placed this book in your hands and is so excited about the healing transformation that is taking place in your life. I am excited for you too! It takes a lot to look so deep within yourself and to challenge wrong thinking and to embrace God's principles and truths. I'm proud of you for the work you have done and am looking forward to the days of healing yet to come for you!

DAY #14
Keep your hand open.

But when you are praying, first forgive anyone you are holding a grudge against, so that your Father in heaven will forgive your sins, too.
— Mark 11:25

IN LIFE WE ARE SOMETIMES blessed with a sincere apology and sometimes we are not. Let us reflect on our Lord's words. Though He did not receive an apology from those who beat Him and were taking His life, He set a perfect example for us.

When they came to the place called the Skull, they crucified him there, along with the criminals—one on his right, the other on his left. Jesus said, "Father, forgive them, for they do not know what they are doing." And they divided up his clothes by casting lots. The people stood watching, and the rulers even sneered at him. They said, "He saved others; let him save himself if he is God's Messiah, the Chosen One." The soldiers also came up and mocked him. They offered him wine vinegar and said, "If you are the king of the Jews, save yourself." There was a written notice above him, which read: this is the king of the Jews. — Luke 23:33-38

Though Christ had been beaten and was among His last breaths, the example of forgiveness He has set is beautiful indeed. He didn't retaliate; yet, He did look deeper into the matter, and He realized that they truly did not understand the magnitude of what they were doing. I think this is true for most people. When someone hurts you, they do not really understand the depth of the pain they are causing. Sometimes we may not even realize how deeply we have been hurt until some time passes and we may begin to act differently toward life and people in general.

There is a weight that comes from resenting someone and not forgiving them and that is a weight that God does not want you to carry.

Whether your pain was inflicted intentionally or unintentionally, I know that you hurt, but do you know that holding on to the hurtful things someone has done only prolongs the pain? It does. The truth is that what's done is already done, and you can't change history at this point. The best you can do is seek healing today and invest in a better tomorrow. Whoever has hurt you may or may not be remorseful or repentant for it, but your healing is not dependent upon them. God is their judge and your redeemer. He is the only one who can bring a healing that is sustainable to the core of your soul, mind, and body. My encouragement for you today is to release the one who has hurt you and to forgive them. I am not saying that what they did is okay or right in any way; it is never okay to hurt people or to abuse them in any way. I am saying that we all have a human nature that is inclined to sin and to be selfish. As long as you think about what has happened to you over and over again and how wrong this person or people are, you are held captive by the event and by them. It is time to let their deeds be judged by God and to rest in knowing that God is able to do what needs to be done on your behalf where they are concerned. Forgive them, for they are imperfect, sinful people and they are not worthy of the energy any longer that you are using in your mind and heart to keep up with them. We are all capable of doing terrible things, and we all need forgiveness. Today, will you make the choice to forgive your offender and trust God to work this out for your good? This is such a critical part to your healing, and I know that with God's help you can do this. It's time.

I encourage you now to forgive your offender to the best of your ability, just as God has forgiven you. Turn everyone involved over to God and let Him bring even deeper healing to your soul as you do.

PLEASE WRITE OUT A PRAYER OF FORGIVENESS BETWEEN YOU AND GOD AND CALL THE PEOPLE WHO HURT YOU BY NAME IN THIS PRAYER. IF THIS FEELS TOO HARD, PLEASE MOVE ON TO THE ACTION PART OF TODAY'S JOURNEY AND THEN COME BACK HERE AFTER YOU ARE DONE.

_____

_____

_____

_____

_____

_____

_____

_____

_____

_____

_____

_____

I am so proud of you. I know we naturally want to nurse our wounds and not allow someone to clean them out. Today the Holy Spirit wants to do just that for you. As you have released the people or person involved, you have removed the greatest obstacle to your healing.

HEALING IN ACTION FOR TODAY

Today you will need a tissue of some sort for this exercise. You will also need your gloves and blanket that you used before.

Let us proceed.

Please get your gloves back out again. The piece of paper that holds the name of your offender should still be in there. Now, get the blanket you have been using as a symbol of God's arms and presence, and wrap it around your shoulders. Ask the precious Holy Spirit to join you; He was sent to comfort you for times such as this.

Place your hands in the gloves, and again I ask that you allow these gloves to represent the hands of Jesus. These hands bled precious holy blood for you and for the one whose name is written on this piece of paper. If forgiving this person(s) is hard, ask Jesus whose nail-scarred hands you are holding to give you strength and remember all the things He has forgiven you for. When you have forgiven to the best of your ability, please take the paper out of the glove and place it in the tissue I asked you to get earlier. Then fold the tissue around the piece of paper and place it to the side. If you are crying, I suggest that you wipe the tears with these gloves you are wearing and allow Jesus to lovingly wipe away your tears. Now, take the tissue and throw it in the trash.

MAKE THIS YOUR PERSONAL DECLARATION TODAY:

Thank you God for forgiving me of my sins and wrongdoings. As freely as you have forgiven me Lord, I choose to forgive _____ _____. I set them free. They owe me nothing and I place them in your hands. God I trust you for everything and thank you for how you will use this for good in my life!

HERE ARE A FEW VERSES I WOULD LIKE YOU TO MEDITATE ON TODAY:

But when you are praying, first forgive anyone you are holding a grudge against, so that your Father in heaven will forgive your sins, too. — Mark 11:25

If you forgive those who sin against you, your heavenly Father will forgive you. — Matthew 6:14

"Thus you shall say to Joseph, "Please forgive, I beg you, the transgression of

your brothers and their sin, for they did you wrong."' And now, please forgive the transgression of the servants of the God of your father." And Joseph wept when they spoke to him. — Genesis 50:17

And forgive us our sins, as we have forgiven those who sin against us. — Matthew 6:12

FROM MY HEART TO YOURS:

God will work everything out for your good; every pain and experience you have endured will never be wasted. Allowing Him the opportunity to make good out of this is your part and the end result is His. It is often   out of our greatest disappointments and fears that ministries and testimonies are birthed. As you have given all things over to Him, you will see that He is going to do amazing things and that He will yet again receive glory and praise. You don't need to worry about how God will do this; you just need to trust that He will. He is working things out on your behalf and in time you will see that this is so.

When you are tempted to resent those involved, again remind yourself that you have forgiven them and that you are all in God's hands.

MY PRAYER FOR YOU TODAY:

Dear LORD, thank you for forgiving us when we ask you. Thank you for sending Jesus so that we ourselves can receive the forgiveness we need and for giving us a tangible example of how this is done. Thank you for helping your child today to release those who have hurt them. I ask that you would use this pain that they have been enduring for the glory of your kingdom and you would work all of this out for their ultimate good. We trust you to do what needs to be done on their behalf and to show us at the appointed time your hand at work in this circumstance. In Jesus' name we release the pain and accept your strength and joy. Amen.

DAY #15
Let's look through the rubble.

Nevertheless, I will bring health and healing to it; I will heal my people and will let them enjoy abundant peace and security. I will bring Judah and Israel back from captivity and will rebuild them as they were before. I will cleanse them from all the sin they have committed against me and will forgive all their sins of rebellion against me. Then this city will bring me renown, joy, praise and honor before all nations on earth that hear of all the good things I do for it; and they will be in awe and will tremble at the abundant prosperity and peace I provide for it. — Jeremiah 33:6-9

ANY TIME WE EXPERIENCE TRAUMA or pain, it can feel like we have been though a disaster of sorts; I will liken it to an earthquake. Do you feel as if you have been though an earthquake? As you look at your life and this difficulty, your heart may feel like it's been shaken, broken, perhaps even shattered, and you may be wondering what you will do with these broken or shattered pieces. In your mind it may look like rubble after an earthquake. I want to encourage you today that not all is rubble or damaged goods. Today I want you to look through what may feel like rubble in your heart and see what may be covered or buried and is of good use and great value. It may take a little digging, but good can still be found and happy is the one who finds it! There are many good things about you and within you to be found and discovered. I encourage you to search for them as you would buried treasure.

Looking at your experience; what positive things have you learned about yourself? If you can't think of anything, please pause and ask the Lord to help you see with His eyes.

LIST SOME THINGS FOR ME:

_____

_____

_____

_____

_____

_____

_____

WHAT DO YOU HAVE THAT WAS NOT TAKEN AWAY FROM YOU? FOR EXAMPLE: YOUR HEALTH, YOUR FRIENDS, A LOVED ONE, A PET, YOUR MEMORIES, YOUR HOME, ETC.

_____

_____

_____

_____

_____

_____

WHAT GOOD THINGS HAVE YOU DISCOVERED ABOUT GOD?

_____

_____

_____

_____

_____

_____

_____

MOVING FORWARD, WHAT ARE THREE THINGS YOU HAVE LEARNED NOT TO DO AGAIN OR THREE WAYS THIS COULD HAVE BEEN PREVENTED THAT YOU KNOW OF. (PLEASE SKIP THIS IF IT DOES NOT APPLY TO YOUR SITUATION.)

1. _____

_____

_____

2. _____

_____

_____

3. _____

_____

_____

Now, look at your answers and see for yourself that good can be found in the rubble. It is with these things that I wish to give you a starting place for rebuilding from the broken or shattered pieces of your heart. It is through the very things you listed that I wish for you to see that not all is wasted if we can learn from our experiences and if we allow ourselves to look for the good. The choice is yours: either look, focus, and cherish the good, or look, focus, and dwell on the bad. It's all really about perspective and the way you choose to see what you hold in your hand.

I wish to remind you today though that God is the Master at taking what we give Him and doing something wonderful with it. Let us remember the little boy with the two fish and the five loaves of bread and how Jesus blessed the gift and fed five thousand. (Read Mark 6:30-44.) Let us also remember Jesus' first miracle and how he helped turn a potentially disgraceful situation for a bridegroom into a miracle as well by turning water into wine for his guests. (Read John 2:1-12.)

There are too many stories to share here, but your Bible is full of truthful accounts of God doing miracles with the simple things we have in our lives every day. He is no respecter of persons and He can do the same for you my friend. Not only can He do these things, but He wants to do them.

MAKE THIS YOUR DECLARATION FOR TODAY AND SAY IT OUT LOUD:

All is not lost! My Redeemer lives! I praise God for the good work He is doing in me! I believe that my best days are yet to come! My purpose is great, and I am an overcomer through Christ Jesus my Lord!

HERE ARE A FEW VERSES I WOULD LIKE YOU TO MEDITATE ON TODAY:

Finally, brothers and sisters, whatever is true, whatever is noble, whatever is right, whatever is pure, whatever is lovely, whatever is admirable—if anything is excellent or praiseworthy—think about such things. — Philippians 4:8

They will say, 'This desolate land has become like the garden of Eden; and the waste, desolate and ruined cities are fortified and inhabited.' Then the nations that are left round about you will know that I, the LORD, have rebuilt the ruined places and planted that which was desolate; I, the LORD, have spoken and will do it." Thus says the Lord GOD, "This also I will let the house of Israel ask Me to do for them: I will increase their men like a flock. — Ezekiel 36:35-37

I will give you hidden treasures, riches stored in secret places, so that you may know that I am the LORD, the God of Israel, who summons you by name. — Isaiah 45:3

*For the Lord gives wisdom;
from his mouth come knowledge and understanding.
He holds success in store for the upright,*

he is a shield to those whose walk is blameless,
for he guards the course of the just
and protects the way of his faithful ones. — Proverbs 2:6-8

FROM MY HEART TO YOURS:

I too have been very well acquainted with the pain of a shattered and broken heart. I know how it feels to be numb because of the pain and even angry beyond belief. As I have healed though and looked through my own rubble with God's help, I have discovered many good things about myself, about God, and about life. I have been able to help thousands and I believe that somehow, someway, you will be making a significant difference in your part of the world as well. You see, I have had the same choice as you to go through my rubble and to my amazement, when I began to look for the good, much was found! I believe the same is true for you: much good is still yet to be found.

MY PRAYER FOR YOU TODAY:

Lord of the universe, Lord of the sky, and Lord of the seas, of every created and living thing, I bless your holy name. You are wonderful in all your ways, and we thank you for today and for helping us to look through the rubble of this difficult situation and find what is good. I pray that you will continue to show your precious child the good in themselves, the good in life, and how very unconditionally you love them. Bless them my Lord, bind up the broken pieces of their heart, and heal them for your name's sake, for we trust in you. Please take the pain and use it on purpose to bring love, compassion, and goodness to those around them in the days and years to come. We praise you today God, because you are good and because your mercies endure forever. In Jesus' name, amen.

DAY #16

Your life is a very precious gift from God!

For those God foreknew he also predestined to be conformed to the image
of his Son, that he might be the firstborn among many brothers and sisters.
And those he predestined, he also called; those he called, he also justified;
those he justified, he also glorified. What, then, shall we say in response to
these things? If God is for us, who can be against us? He who did not spare his
own Son, but gave him up for us all—how will he not also, along with him,
graciously give us all things?
— Romans 8:29-32

YOU ARE SO VERY PRECIOUS to God. Before you were formed, He knew you and had great plans for you. I want to encourage you today in the truth that God is the one who validates your existence, your gifts and talents, and the approval your heart is longing for. Regardless of what anyone else may believe or say, what God says and ordains prevails. Unfortunately some people at times would like for us to give up on life and doubt that we are worth anything at all. This simply is not so! God has always wanted you here, and that's why you are here. He has created good works for you to carry out and has given you gifts and talents for this very special life of yours. God is for you, so fear not and fret not for who may be against you. They are temporal in this world, and God is eternal.

It is important that we silence the lies, the voices in our minds, and the negative thoughts we have believed about ourselves, which derived from people or from difficult circumstances in life. These are all destructive and contrary to God's Word. We have already established that Jehovah God has the highest authority anywhere, that His words are true, that we trust in Him, and that our lives are in His hands. When He says that He has a plan for you, and that it's good, He means just that! When He says His thoughts toward you are good, and that they outnumber the sand on the seashore, He means just that! When He says that He has called you by name, justified you, and made you right with Him though the sacrifice of His Son, He means just that. When He says that nothing will ever be able to separate you from His love, He means just that! When He says that you are forgiven, He means just that! It is up to you to believe those words though and to give them more weight and value than words that you may hear that put you down, crush your spirit, and defeat you! The choice is yours. You can allow the hurtful words of others or destructive thoughts of your own to fill your mind, or you can fill your mind with the loving, powerful, and authoritative words of God. The thing you cannot afford to do is be double-minded. Choose for yourself who you will allow to have the greatest influence on your identity and worth, and then stick to it and move on. Your life is precious to the Lord, and there is not another like you. He has taken great time and loving care in creating your personality, looks, talents, and abilities. He loves it when you come to Him with a childlike faith and simply believe what He tells you and then live like you believe Him.

PLEASE WRITE DOWN LIES, THOUGHTS, OR BELIEFS THAT HAVE HELD YOU BACK FROM ENJOYING YOUR LIFE OR MOVING FORWARD.

_____

_____

_____

_____

_____

_____

_____

_____

_____

_____

_____

_____

_____

Now confess those things to the Lord and ask Him to help you believe His truths about you, your life, and your future.

Today, choose to believe that God has a great plan for your life and that He is not limited by the hurtful experience you have been through. He is not limited by other people's negative perceptions or opinions of you either. He has given you your life as a precious gift, and He would like for you to enjoy it, live righteously, and use it for good. Will you accept His gift today?

PLEASE WRITE THAT OUT IN A PRAYER HERE AND THANK HIM FOR HIS APPROVAL. HE LIKES YOU! THANK HIM FOR MAKING YOU RIGHT BEFORE

HIM BECAUSE OF THE PERFECT SACRIFICE OF HIS SON JESUS CHRIST. THANK HIM FOR CHOOSING YOU TO BE HIS AND FOR GIVING YOU THE GIFT OF LIFE TO ENJOY AND TO MAKE A DIFFERENCE IN THE WORLD WITH.

_____

_____

_____

_____

_____

_____

_____

_____

_____

_____

_____

HERE ARE A FEW VERSES I WOULD LIKE YOU TO MEDITATE ON TODAY:

Now the word of the LORD came to me saying, "Before I formed you in the womb I knew you, And before you were born I consecrated you; I have appointed you a prophet to the nations." — Jeremiah 1:4-5

"For I know the plans I have for you," says the LORD. "They are plans for good and not for disaster, to give you a future and a hope." — Jeremiah 29:11

How precious also are Your thoughts to me, O God! How vast is the sum of them! If I should count them, they would outnumber the sand. When I awake, I am still with You. — Psalm 139:17-18

God is not human, that he should lie, not a human being, that he should change his mind. Does he speak and then not act? Does he promise and not fulfill? — Numbers 23:19

For we are God's handiwork, created in Christ Jesus to do good works, which God prepared in advance for us to do. — Ephesians 2:10

Now, this is what the Lord says—
he who created you, Jacob,
he who formed you, Israel:
"Do not fear, for I have redeemed you;

I have summoned you by name; you are mine.
When you pass through the waters,
I will be with you;
and when you pass through the rivers,
they will not sweep over you.
When you walk through the fire,
you will not be burned;
the flames will not set you ablaze.
For I am the Lord your God,
the Holy One of Israel, your Savior;
I give Egypt for your ransom,
Cush and Seba in your stead.
Since you are precious and honored in my sight,
and because I love you,
I will give people in exchange for you,
nations in exchange for your life.
Do not be afraid, for I am with you;
I will bring your children from the east
and gather you from the west.
I will say to the north, 'Give them up!'
and to the south, 'Do not hold them back.'
Bring my sons from afar
and my daughters from the ends of the earth—
everyone who is called by my name,
whom I created for my glory,
whom I formed and made." — Isaiah 43:1-7

MAKE THIS YOUR PERSONAL DECLARATION TODAY AND SAY IT OUT LOUD:

I have been created on purpose and for a good purpose by God Almighty. I will enjoy my life and bless God with it. I believe His words are true, His thoughts toward me are good, and that He enjoys my company. No weapon formed against me will prosper, and every tongue that rises up against me will be put to shame in Jesus' name!

MY PRAYER FOR YOU TODAY:

Father, how marvelous are your ways. How majestic is your voice. How beautiful is your heart toward this child of yours. I pray oh Father that today you will heal them even deeper and help them to embrace your thoughts of love and acceptance for them. Protect them in every way possible. Help them to believe you with a childlike faith, in Jesus' name, amen.

FROM MY HEART TO YOURS:

Friend, look how far you have come in this journey! You have grown by leaps and bounds, and I am so proud of you! I trust that today you are feeling stronger and encouraged by the Father's words that I have brought to your attention. I believe He wants you to live a life filled with hope and a heart filled with peace. Your life is precious, and I'm looking forward to hearing from you personally as to how this book has impacted your life!

DAY #17
Be vigilant and on guard!

Above all else, guard your heart, for everything you do flows from it.
— Proverbs 4:23

YOUR HEART IS THE ESSENCE of who you are. The condition of your heart correlates directly to the condition of your life and how you live it. From a strong and healthy heart comes passion, zeal, excellence, dreams, courage, perseverance, joy, hope, love, gratitude, and a multitude of other positive emotions and actions. When these wonderful things are present, life feels great, satisfying, and enjoyable. I believe that everyone enjoys living life this way! This is a result of a heart that is being intentionally cared for. One that is well-guarded and well-invested in. In life though, hard times come, and if we have not been diligent in guarding our heart, we can find ourselves with a heart that is weak, and from the weak heart flows sorrow, despair, bitterness, jealousy, strife, fear, loneliness, desperation, anxiety, poor work performance, and even laziness at times. This is not an enjoyable way to live life for any of us. When we feel this way, it's hard to get up in the morning, to feel motivated, and at times to even care about living at all. When this is the case, we lose valuable time in life, and we are robbed of the beautiful gift of life given to us by our loving Heavenly Father. This is the reason we are encouraged to guard out hearts in Proverbs 4:23. Your heart is precious, priceless, and irreplaceable. It is entrusted primarily to you, and you alone. Understanding that you are to guard it as one guarding anything of great value, such as a crown, a painting, a person, or even a nation, is wise.

CAN YOU DESCRIBE THE GOOD QUALITIES OF YOUR HEART TO ME? PLEASE DO SO HERE:

_____

_____

_____

_____

_____

_____

_____

THANK YOU. NOW PLEASE DESCRIBE HOW YOU WERE GUARDING YOUR HEART WHEN YOUR HURTFUL EXPERIENCE HAPPENED AND EVEN LEADING UP TO THE EXPERIENCE.

_____

_____

_____

_____

_____

_____

Today, I desire to encourage you to be diligent in guarding your heart. Live your life as one who understands the value you possess within yourself. You are valuable, precious, and inhabited by the Spirit of the Living God. You are a child of God. He qualifies you as one that is of great worth and value, which is seen by the sacrifice He made in sending His one and only beloved Son Jesus Christ to die in place of you spiritually for all eternity. Consider this: when you are honored, so is He as He abides in you. When you are dishonored, so is He as He abides in you. Learning to guard your heart is essential for your wellbeing, and it will help you to produce good fruit in your life. Consider the following as good ways to guard your heart.

1. Refuse to allow negative or hurtful words that are spoken to you or about you, to penetrate or remain with you. Refuse to think about them all day/ night long! Cast them down and do not accept them as unchanging truth. Confess God's Word as truth instead.

2. Set realistic expectations for the people you are in relationship with. For example, do not expect unbelievers to act like Christians. Do not expect tender words from people who are generally harsh in their speech. Do not expect understanding from those who may not seem genuinely interested in you. People cannot give you anything they do not have. Wishing they would be something that they are not is harmful to you and to them.

3. Set boundaries of respect and truth in your life. Evaluate what you need from those you are in relationship with and clearly communicate that to them. Be willing to reexamine the relationships you have that cannot or will not honor your boundaries.

4. Invest in yourself by taking time to be alone with the Lord and allowing Him to minister to you. Give Him the highest priority in your life by

sharing time with Him and guarding that time diligently, ensuring that it happens on a daily basis.

5. Be in tune with the Holy Spirit and His promptings. Obey quickly and do not forfeit your peace by ignoring His voice.

6. Get plenty of rest so that you can replenish the strength you are using in life. A tired, weary body and mind will greatly affect your heart.

7. Invest quality time in your most cherished relationships. Try not to take those you genuinely love and those who love you in return for granted. Spend your energy and time giving and receiving love here. Listen to them, share with them, and communicate with appropriate vulnerability in proportion to how they have shown themselves to be trustworthy. Do not neglect spending time with them and intentionally be very present when you do.

8. Do not shift the responsibility of guarding your heart and making it a number one priority to someone else, understanding that it is yours and yours alone to make as your number one priority.

9. Be careful not to treat your heart casually, as if it has no value or little value at all. You alone know the truth about how loyal, tender, kind, forgiving, trusting, compassionate, and genuine you are, and these things are very valuable. So, be careful to guard those precious qualities of your heart.

10. Invest in yourself by engaging in recreational activities that rejuvenate you, like reading, cooking, scrapbooking, fishing, writing, playing sports, playing music, etc. Being able to expend energy on things you enjoy is both fun and emotionally beneficial.

When you understand the great worth of your heart and how the condition of it affects everything in your life, then you should be mindful of how well it needs to be guarded. Be vigilant and be careful not to fall asleep on this job.

HOW CAN YOU BE A BETTER STEWARD OF YOUR HEART? ANSWER HERE:

_____

_____

_____

_____

_____

_____

_____

_____

_____

_____

_____

HERE ARE A FEW VERSES I WOULD LIKE YOU TO MEDITATE ON TODAY:

Do not give dogs what is sacred; do not throw your pearls to pigs. If you do, they may trample them under their feet, and turn and tear you to pieces. — Matthew 7:6

Above all else, guard your heart, for everything you do flows from it. — Proverbs 4:23

Listen, my son, and be wise, and set your heart on the right path. — Proverbs 23:19

Don't befriend angry people or associate with hot-tempered people. — Proverbs 22:24

Very early in the morning, while it was still dark, Jesus got up, left the house and went off to a solitary place, where he prayed. — Mark 1:35

Don't you realize that all of you together are the temple of God and that the Spirit of God lives in you? — 1 Corinthians 3:16

MY PRAYER FOR YOU TODAY:

Father, thank you for loving us and for causing our paths to cross. You are so faithful and so loving Father, and always giving us just what we need when we need it. I come before you now asking for you to bless this child of yours, to impart to them wisdom, grace, and truth. Protect them and the things they have purposed in their heart today. Grant them understanding and strength for the task of guarding their hearts my Lord. Help them as they incline their ears to you and seek to live a holy life, a joyful life, and a productive life for you, in Jesus' name, amen.

MAKE THIS YOUR PERSONAL DECLARATION TODAY:

I am strong in the Lord and the power of His might. I will be diligent in guarding my heart, honoring myself, and honoring Christ in me. I am the Father's beloved, and He is mine.

FROM MY HEART TO YOURS:

Thank you for trusting me on this journey with your heart. I want to encourage you to assign great value to what God has done within you and eagerly anticipate the good that He is still yet to do. Honoring the good in you is so important. Honoring Christ in you is as well. Not everyone in your life is going to celebrate you or appreciate the beauty of what lies under your skin, and that is okay. Celebrate who you are and cherish the good regardless. Look to God for validation before anyone else and seek His face for the deep intimacy your heart is longing for. He is right there with you now, and oh how He loves you and longs to be your number one love in life.

For the ones who have failed to see your worth, I am sorry. For the ones who took you for granted, I am sorry. For the ones who robbed you of your kindness, I am sorry. For the one who has betrayed you, I am sorry. For the one who overlooked you, I am sorry. For the one who has left you feeling worthless, I am sorry. For the one who has left you, I am sorry. Please know that with God by your side, you have One who sees your worth, One who does not take you for granted, One who will never rob you, One who will never betray you, One who will never overlook you, One who will never hurt you and leave you feeling worthless, One who will always remain by your side. Please take these words to heart and allow them to sink deep into your soul today.

HEALING IN ACTION FOR TODAY

Today I would like you to create a heart out of any material you like. You can draw, color, paint, mold, or chisel wood in the image of a heart, which is to be symbolic of your heart to you. On this heart, place the words you wrote about the good in it. Then place it where you will see it on a daily basis as a reminder of your charge to guard it and to guard it well.

DAY #18

May your spring give fresh water.

With the tongue we praise our Lord and Father, and with it we curse human beings, who have been made in God's likeness. Out of the same mouth come praise and cursing. My brothers and sisters, this should not be. Can both fresh water and salt water flow from the same spring? My brothers and sisters, can a fig tree bear olives, or a grapevine bear figs? Neither can a salt spring produce fresh water. — James 3:9-12

YOUR WORDS HAVE POWER AND will make a big impact on your life and in the situation you are working through. Your words are like water, either bitter, clean, polluted, sweet, pure, muddy, or destructive even, at times. Of this water you will drink, and so will those around you. Have you ever considered drinking water that was contaminated with poison? I hope not. You're too important and the Father has need of you! I hope that when you are thirsty and need a drink of water that you are reaching for nice clean and cool water, water that will refresh and replenish you. Likewise I hope that when you talk about yourself that you are speaking words that give life, ones that are edifying, and ones that line up with what God says about you.

When we have been hurt, it is tempting to talk about the situation over and over again when it's not really needed and then when we talk about it, the words we speak can be negative or lead to destruction. It can be to the person(s) whom you have already forgiven, or to the one listening as they listen to how you are living your life, or to yourself. Especially when it causes you to relive yet again the hurt, pain, and sorrow you have been working so hard to move through. It is best if your words are well thought out and ones that bring God and His truths into your story. Being intentional with what you say is key. Speak with victory over your circumstances, understanding that your words are influential and that they contain power in them. The Spirit of God dwells in you, and you want to guard your mouth so that you do not grieve the Holy Spirit and at the same time lose your peace. When you begin to speak in a negative manner, you underestimate and withdraw the testimony of God's healing power that is present in your life. When you speak in faith, it pleases God, for without faith, it is impossible to please Him. It also strengthens you as you listen to your own words and influence your heart and the hearts around you. God is alive and He says that He watches over His Word to perform it. His words will not return to Him void. You can be assured that by the word of your testimony you will overcome. You may not have the outcome you desired in this situation, or you may fear the outcome that is to come; however, it is important that you hold fast to your confession of victory. You can be confident in declaring your victory because God will work everything out for your good. He says so in Romans 8:28: And we know that in all things God works for the good of those who love him, who have been called according to his purpose.

A good outcome is what will await you both now and in the future.

When talking about your situation, have you been using words such as: I can't, I don't know how, I give up, or I hate?

THINK ABOUT THAT FOR A MINUTE AND WRITE DOWN NEGATIVE THINGS YOU HAVE BEEN SAYING.

_____

_____

_____

_____

_____

_____

_____

_____

Those words are defeating, and it's time to stop using them!

NOW, I WANT YOU TO REWRITE WHAT YOU JUST WROTE DOWN WITH WORDS OF FAITH AND WORDS FROM THE PERSPECTIVE OF AN OVERCOMER.

_____

_____

_____

_____

_____

_____

_____

Good job! Now, rehearse these things in your mind and begin using them rather than the negative and defeating words you have been using when talking about yourself or the situation.

HERE ARE A FEW VERSES I WOULD LIKE YOU TO MEDITATE ON TODAY:

When we put bits into the mouths of horses to make them obey us, we can turn the whole animal. Or take ships as an example. Although they are so large and are driven by strong winds, they are steered by a very small rudder wherever the pilot wants to go. Likewise, the tongue is a small part of the body, but it makes great boasts. Consider what a great forest is set on fire by a small spark. The tongue also is a fire, a world of evil among the parts of the body. It corrupts the whole body, sets the whole course of one's life on fire, and is itself set on fire by hell. — James 3:3-6

For the director of music. For Jeduthun. A psalm of David. I said, "I will watch my ways and keep my tongue from sin; I will put a muzzle on my mouth while in the presence of the wicked." — Psalm 39:1

Those who consider themselves religious and yet do not keep a tight rein on their tongues deceive themselves, and their religion is worthless. — James 1:26

Set a guard over my mouth, LORD; keep watch over the door of my lips. — Psalm 141:3

I call heaven and earth to witness against you today, that I have set before you life and death, the blessing and the curse. So choose life in order that you may live, you and your descendants, by loving the LORD your God, by obeying His voice, and by holding fast to Him; for this is your life and the length of your days, that you may live in the land which the LORD swore to your fathers, to Abraham, Isaac, and Jacob, to give them. — Deuteronomy 30:19-20

And without faith it is impossible to please Him, for he who comes to God must believe that He is and that He is a rewarder of those who seek Him. — Hebrews 11:6

MAKE THIS YOUR DECLARATION:

I will bless the Lord at all times and His praises shall continuously be on my lips. I am blessed of the Lord; goodness and mercy will follow me all the days of my life. I am above and not beneath. I am the head and not the tail. I live in victory every day, and God is with me everywhere I go.

HEALING IN ACTION FOR TODAY

Please say these words out loud and let them resonate in your heart, mind, and soul.

- I am a sanctified saint in Jesus Christ (1 Corinthians 1:2).

- I am in Christ who gives me wisdom, righteousness, sanctification, and redemption (1 Corinthians 1:30).

- I am blessed with every spiritual blessing in the heavenly places in Christ. (Ephesians 1:3)

- I am the light of the world (Matthew 5:14).

- I am the sweet aroma of Christ (2 Corinthians 2:16).

- I am being transformed into the likeness of the Lord ever increasingly with glory from God (2 Corinthians 5:17).

- I am an heir of God and fellow heir with Christ (Romans 8:17).

- I am a chosen race, a royal priesthood, a holy nation, a person for God's own possession, that I may proclaim the excellences of Him who has called me out of darkness and into His marvelous light (1 Peter 2:9).

MY PRAYER FOR YOU TODAY:

Lord, thank you that you invite us to choose life, and today we choose to live life according to your instructions. I ask oh Lord, that you will bless and protect your child. I ask that you would set a guard on their mouths and that their mouths will speak words of edification and faith. I pray that you will help them to be keenly aware of what they are saying and that you will help them exercise wisdom in their speech. Add to them a zeal for life, a passion for seeking you, and strength for the work of your kingdom. I pray in Jesus' name.

FROM MY HEART TO YOURS:

It can be easy to form a right habit in place of a wrong one. Choosing your words wisely will help to keep you from defeating yourself and taking away from your testimony of victory. You are destined for greatness, and it's important that your mouth confesses that. Making a choice to speak words of edification and faith will help you gain new ground in your healing journey.

DAY #19

What is on your mind?

For the weapons of our warfare are not of the flesh, but divinely powerful for the destruction of fortresses. We are destroying speculations and every lofty thing raised up against the knowledge of God, and we are taking every thought captive to the obedience of Christ. — 2 Corinthians 10:4

GOD HAS GIVEN YOU A beautiful mind. He has wonderfully created you to think, feel, and to have free will. His intentions for you are good and they come from His heart of love. As we have journeyed together, we have contemplated many things, let go of things, and picked up hope along the way. I trust that your mind has been renewed day by day. As I have encouraged you to be vigilant about guarding your heart and mouth, I also want to encourage you to do so with your mind. Your mind is a battlefield of sorts where thoughts are firing off all day long. Some are good and some are bad, and oftentimes they war with each other. I want to encourage you to pay attention to what you're thinking about. It can be easy to get caught up with a negative conversation in your mind, and that conversation will bring your heart down. It's time to exercise stopping those conversations and daydreams at their onset. You must not allow your mind to get carried away, or you will find yourself struggling to overcome your experience. You can take every thought you have captive to the obedience of Jesus Christ. When you find yourself thinking negatively toward yourself, or toward others who have hurt you, or constantly repeating the hurtful events that have happened, you must try to quickly bring them to a stop. The quicker you stop them, the less power they will have over your mind, will, and emotions. You do not have to entertain every thought that comes to your mind. If it is not beneficial or edifying, stop it and let it go. In your mind, I would like you to imagine putting a handcuff on that thought and bringing it to Jesus. Repent quickly for allowing yourself to entertain it, receive His forgiveness, and go on with your day. Making a conscience decision to limit the amount of space you will give this hurtful experience and pain is key to moving forward. You do have control over this, though you may not have had control over the hurtful experience. I want you to know that you are empowered to take control of your thought life. Do not allow yourself to rehearse the past of painful memories over and over again. The more you practice stopping negative thoughts, the quicker you will get at it.

How often do you find yourself thinking in a way that needs to be stopped? Today make a commitment to yourself and to God to take control of wandering thoughts. Just because a thought comes to mind does not mean that you must entertain it.

PLEASE SHARE YOUR THOUGHTS HERE ON THIS CONCEPT.

_____
_____
_____
_____
_____
_____
_____
_____
_____
_____
_____
_____
_____
_____
_____
_____
_____
_____

WHAT ARE SOME POSITIVE AND SCRIPTURAL THOUGHTS YOU CAN COMBAT NEGATIVE THOUGHTS WITH WHEN YOUR MIND GETS CARRIED AWAY IN A NEGATIVE SPIRAL DOWN? TRY TO LIST FIVE.

1._____
_____
2._____
_____
3._____
_____

4._____

_____

5._____

_____

It's important for you to understand that what you allow will continue. So do not allow yourself to become a casualty of the negative war that can go in in your mind. You can do this! You may get tired of fighting this battle, but do not quit! Satan often attacks here so that he can build a fortress and make himself a home. Remember that this place belongs to you though, and that you are not alone in the battles. God's Spirit dwells in you, and He will help you. He is with you as your helper and He loves doing just that, helping you. You have your part to do, and God has His part to do, and together you are a mighty!

HERE ARE A FEW VERSES I WOULD LIKE YOU TO MEDITATE ON TODAY:

Let the peace of Christ rule in your hearts, to which indeed you were called in one body; and be thankful. Let the word of Christ richly dwell within you, with all wisdom teaching and admonishing one another with psalms and hymns and spiritual songs, singing with thankfulness in your hearts to God. Whatever you do in word or deed, do all in the name of the Lord Jesus, giving thanks through Him to God the Father. — Colossians 3:15-17

And now, dear brothers and sisters, one final thing. Fix your thoughts on what is true, and honorable, and right, and pure, and lovely, and admirable. Think about things that are excellent and worthy of praise. — Philippians 4:8

But the wisdom from above is first of all pure. It is also peace loving, gentle at all times, and willing to yield to others. It is full of mercy and good deeds. It shows no favoritism and is always sincere. — James 3:17

The thief's purpose is to steal and kill and destroy. My purpose is to give them a rich and satisfying life. — John 10:10

MY PRAYER FOR YOU TODAY:

I thank you Lord for this beautiful day that you have made, for the life you have given to this your precious child, and for the good mind you have equipped them with. I give you praise, for you are marvelous in all your ways. You are generous and faithful and always good. I pray my precious Lord that you will bless this precious one and help them to bring every thought captive to you. Help them to be quick to capture their thoughts and not to let their thoughts cause them to drift back into the depth of the pain they have experienced. I thank you that day by day you are making them whole and taking them from glory to glory! I thank you that day by day they are resembling you more and being transformed into your image. Take this work they have done and seal it for the glory of your name and for the sake of your child. We give you praise for always being so faithful to help us and for granting us your words of wisdom and truth, in Jesus' name, amen.

MAKE THIS YOUR DECLARATION TODAY:

I am able to do all things through Christ who gives me strength. I will take every negative and defeating thought I have to Jesus and entertain them no more. I am blessed, highly favored, and chosen by God, and will be used for His glory in Jesus' name!

FROM MY HEART TO YOURS:

Dear one, the victory is yours! As you gain strength here, you will also gain freedom. I am so proud of you and how far you have come on this journey! Day by day, as you embrace your new strength, I hope you are smiling and laughing more. I hope you are able to see more good and beauty around you and I hope you are loving this book! When I think of you doing those very things, it brings the biggest smile to my face. You are dearly loved by your Lord and compassionately thought of by me.

DAY #20

Practice, practice, practice!

"I am the vine; you are the branches. If you remain in me and I in you, you will bear much fruit; apart from me you can do nothing. If you do not remain in me, you are like a branch that is thrown away and withers; such branches are picked up, thrown into the fire and burned. If you remain in me and my words remain in you, ask whatever you wish, and it will be done for you. This is to my Father's glory, that you bear much fruit, showing yourselves to be my disciples." — John 15:5-8

DAILY WE ARE CALLED TO take up our cross and follow Jesus. Your cross has probably been heavy at times. So was His. One of the wonderful things about our Lord is that He was 100 percent God, and He was also 100 percent man, and because of that He can understand you and empathize with you. In your journey you have been carrying your cross, and today I want to encourage you to lay it down at the feet of Jesus and to simply enjoy His presence. Acknowledge Him as being right there with you wherever you're at right now.

** Please pause for a moment to do so. **

Moving forward, I want to encourage you to recognize him every day and all day. Invite Him to dine with you whenever you eat. Welcome Him as you are getting ready for the day. Consciously acknowledge Him and His Spirit in your car, when you're outside, at your place of employment, and in every room of your home. Rest in knowing that you are not alone, that He will never abandon you, and that He enjoys your company. Daily He invites you to abide in Him. Abiding in Christ is a willful choice that will yield much good fruit in your life. Fruit such as love, joy peace, patience, kindness, goodness, etc. The way you abide in Him is by acknowledging His presence and communicating with Him moment by moment, day by day. He invites you to share all things with Him, good and bad, that are in your life. He loves it when you come to Him with childlike faith in His love and care, and when you don't run or hide from Him. His desire is always for you to draw closer to Him, not to run far away. I wish to admonish you to daily spend time in reading the Bible and studying His words. Pray and talk to Him all day long and look to Him to guide you and to give you the peace and answers you need in your life. I also wish for you to understand that, the relationship He invites you to enjoy with Him daily is intimate. It's safe. It's optional, and it will satisfy you in a way no other can. He will never force Himself on you and demand your attention. He will gently nudge your heart though and wait for your invitation to join you. He is always ready, always willing, and always dependable. When you spend your days with Him, they will be blessed and graced with peace. I didn't say perfect or without problems, for that time is yet to come when your time here on earth is done. I believe these days of peace are the type of days your soul thirsts for. He knew this and so He has invited you to drink of His living water and to enjoy His company. Daily it will satisfy your soul so that spiritually you will never thirst again. Please realize though that a day lived any differently than this will produce just the opposite. You will feel alone, frustrated, and in search of rest. Beware though because in that search, you can be deceived and tempted to fall for numerous short-term satisfactions. These may bring you quick relief; however, the promises they give are false. These quick fixes can enslave you to sin and bondage to someone or something that will never deeply and truly satisfy the longing of your heart. If you drink of these things, your soul will thirst again.

So, make sure to be vigilant in practicing being in His presence and communing with Him every second of your day. Remain prayerful and conscience of His presence and allow Him the joy of sharing every moment of your life forevermore. Know that He is in all of your tomorrows waiting for you as well.

WRITE OUT A PRAYER HERE SHARING YOUR THOUGHTS WITH HIM ABOUT ABIDING IN HIM AND ENJOYING HIS COMPANY.

_____

_____

_____

_____

_____

_____

_____

_____

_____

_____

_____

_____

_____

_____

PLEASE SHARE WITH ME FIVE WORDS THAT DESCRIBE YOUR FEELINGS AFTER WRITING OUT THAT PRAYER:

1._____

_____

2._____

_____

3._____

_____

4._____

_____

5._____

_____

SCRIPTURES FOR YOU TO MEDITATE ON:

I am the true vine, and my Father is the gardener. He cuts off every branch in me that bears no fruit, while every branch that does bear fruit he prunes so that it will be even more fruitful. You are already clean because of the word I have spoken to you. Remain in me, as I also remain in you. No branch can bear fruit by itself; it must remain in the vine. Neither can you bear fruit unless you remain in me.

I am the vine; you are the branches. If you remain in me and I in you, you will bear much fruit; apart from me you can do nothing. If you do not remain in me, you are like a branch that is thrown away and withers; such branches are picked up, thrown into the fire and burned. If you remain in me and my words remain in you, ask whatever you wish, and it will be done for you. This is to my Father's glory, that you bear much fruit, showing yourselves to be my disciples.

As the Father has loved me, so have I loved you. Now remain in my love. If you keep my commands, you will remain in my love, just as I have kept my Father's commands and remain in his love. I have told you this so that my joy may be in you and that your joy may be complete. My command is this: Love each other as I have loved you. Greater love has no one than this: to lay down one's life for one's friends. You are my friends if you do what I command. I no longer call you servants, because a servant does not know his master's business. Instead, I have called you friends, for everything that I learned from my Father I have made known to you. You did not choose me, but I chose you and appointed you so that you might go and bear fruit—fruit that will last—and so that whatever you ask in my name the Father will give you. This is my command: Love each other." — John 15:1-17

HEALING IN ACTION FOR TODAY

Please get your gloves and allow them to represent the hands of Jesus to you today and wear them off and on throughout the day. Do so as many times as possible to be reminded and encouraged that He is near in all that you do.

MAKE THIS YOUR DECLARATION TODAY:

I am rich in love, I am rich in company, and I am rich in God's favor!

MY PRAYER FOR YOU TODAY:

We love you Lord. Thank you for the pleasure of enjoying your company all day today and in all the days that are yet to come. You are good, and we make you our refuge and dwelling place. We take shelter under the shadow of your wings and delight in knowing you more. Lord, I ask that again you will reveal your nearness to this your precious child and open their eyes that they might see more of you today. As they abide in you, I ask that they would bear much fruit and that you would satisfy their hunger and thirst for joy, peace, and righteousness. In Jesus' name, amen.

FROM MY HEART TO YOURS:

Practicing being in the presence of God is wonderful. It transforms every day and laces it with His grace. Your days spent this way will be more meaningful. They will help you to sharpen your skill of listening to His voice and discerning His will for your life. I am excited about the times you will share with Him and how this will empower you in your life's journey. It has made such a wonderful difference in my life, and to this day I practice being in His presence so much that it feels more normal and comfortable to me than any other relationship I have ever had! God bless you dear one, God bless you.

DAY #21

You are an offering.

Therefore, I urge you, brothers and sisters, in view of God's mercy, to offer your bodies as a living sacrifice, holy and pleasing to God—this is your true and proper worship. — Romans 12:1

GOD IS SO GOOD, SO LOVING, and so kind, and He loves you! He gives so freely, and loves it when you accept His love and enjoy His company. He is holy and worthy of your praise. Have you ever considered how much He has given you and wondered what you could do to show your appreciation? I know I have. In this journey together, I believe that God has given you greater understanding, new hope, healing, strategies for life, a dream for a better future, and a great deal of comfort. As with any good, loving, and healthy relationship, it's important that you invest as well by giving back to Him. Oh, I know that you can't give Him the exact same things in return, but He has not really asked for that from you. He has asked for your love though. He asks for you to have a loving devotion to Him and for you to show your love for Him by loving others. With the comfort He has given you, He wants you to comfort others. When you do this, He accepts it just as if you have done it unto Him.

In this journey and time here in this book with me, you have probably learned or experienced things that others around you need to have as well. Would you share with them? This would be considered an offering. Have you ever thought of giving a kind word to someone as an offering to God? He is worthy of your entire life being an offering. I want to encourage you to offer yourself up to Him and yield your life to His will. Let your mind, body, and spirit be free from sin and as pure as possible. Give Him your very best with each new day that is to come and discover the joy in living your life as an offering for Him. Strive to be spotless before Him and to obey quickly any prompting that He may give you. Let the words of your mouth and the thoughts in your mind be pleasing to Him. This is reasonable for the One who loves you unconditionally, purely, without wavering, and for all eternity. After all He has healed you, forgiven you, bought you with the price of His only begotten Son Jesus Christ, given you His Spirit, and renewed your inner man. He is worthy of all your love and devotion because He has been so loving, gracious, and kind.

Would you commit yourself as an offering to Him today? Will you pour out your love for Him through every breath you take from now on and forevermore?

WRITE OUT YOUR THOUGHTS AS A PRAYER HERE:

_____
_____
_____
_____
_____
_____
_____
_____
_____
_____
_____
_____
_____

What a beautiful thing indeed to dedicate yourself to Him. Nothing you do in His name will ever be forgotten by Him or go unnoticed. I encourage you today to ask God whom you can be a blessing to within the next week as a way of giving back to Him.

I ENCOURAGE YOU TO ASK FOR THREE PEOPLE OR PLACES YOU CAN BE A BLESSING TO AND DO SO IN HONOR OF THE THREE WHO HAVE MINISTERED FREELY TO YOU HERE—THE FATHER, THE SON, AND THE HOLY GHOST.

1._____
_____
_____
_____

2._____
_____
_____
_____

3._____

_____

_____

_____

How exciting and what a privilege it is to serve and to love. What a blessing to be an extension of God's love, grace, and mercy here on earth. Forevermore I hope you will join me in daily bringing Him extravagant worship and love.

> *Brethren, I do not regard myself as having laid hold of it yet; but one thing I do: forgetting what lies behind and reaching forward to what lies ahead, I press on toward the goal for the prize of the upward call of God in Christ Jesus. —* *Philippians 3:13-14*

Here we are on the last day of journey together! I am so excited about what God has done in your heart through this book. I know that you have been set free and are stronger than you were when you began. In understanding that this is the end of our journey together in this book, let us consider it as a new beginning of the next chapter in the rest of your life. God has such amazing plans for you, and I believe your best days are still yet to come. It's very important that as you move forward, you stay focused and keep your mind fixed on Christ. Many things will compete for your attention, and it can be easy to get sidetracked and lose focus if you're not careful. Be vigilant about what you say, what you think about, and guarding your heart. You are so very special and so very important to God and to the work you have been assigned to do in this world. You are here on this earth on purpose and for a great purpose; seek what that is and pursue it diligently and passionately. We must be about our Father's business for the days are short and the fields are ripe unto harvest. Keep your eyes on the prize: the prize of heaven, the prize of the crown of life that you will obtain, the prize of seeing Jesus face to face without shame, and the prize of an eternal life in heaven where you have stored up for yourself treasures that moth cannot eat, treasure that will not be stolen.

REFLECT FOR A MOMENT. THINK ABOUT WHO YOU WERE AND HOW THIS PAIN AFFECTED YOUR LIFE WHEN YOU BEGAN THIS BOOK, AND COMPARE IT TO HOW YOU SEE AND FEEL ABOUT YOURSELF NOW:

_____

_____

_____

_____

_____

_____

_____

_____

_____

_____

_____

_____

_____

_____

_____

_____

_____

_____

_____

I give God glory, honor, and praise with you for the deep healing work He has done in your life. Now, it's time for you to be an encouragement and voice of hope for those around you. Would you consider leading a small group of people in your home, church, community, or place of employment through this? Would you allow God to use your pain to help bring healing to others? Please give that some thought and prayerful consideration.

SCRIPTURES TO MEDITATE ON:

I consider that our present sufferings are not worth comparing with the glory that will be revealed in us. — Romans 8:18

Be thankful in all circumstances, for this is God's will for you who belong to Christ Jesus. — 1 Thessalonians 5:18

For our light and momentary troubles are achieving for us an eternal glory that far outweighs them all. — 2 Corinthians 4:17

When Christ, who is your life, appears, then you also will appear with him in glory. — Colossians 3:4

But rejoice inasmuch as you participate in the sufferings of Christ, so that you may be overjoyed when his glory is revealed. — 1 Peter 4:13

In this you greatly rejoice, even though now for a little while, if necessary, you have been distressed by various trials, so that the proof of your faith, being more precious than gold which is perishable, even though tested by fire, may be found to result in praise and glory and honor at the revelation of Jesus Christ. — 1 Peter 1:6-7

MY CLOSING PRAYER FOR YOU:

My precious Lord, how beautiful and honorable is your name. You alone have the power to save, to heal, to cleanse, and to set free, and this is what I am asking of you for today. Empower this child of yours, heal their innermost being, cleanse them from the pain, and set them completely free from any bondages they may be in. Remove from them the sin, guilt, and shame that has been born by Jesus on the cross. Pour out upon them in a fresh new way your sweet Holy Spirit. Anoint them with the oil of joy and gladness. Strengthen their heart and soul. Captivate them with your presence and your love. Reveal any and all lies conveyed by the father of lies, Satan himself. Let not any of his wicked schemes prevail. Send forth your warring angels to minister on your child's behalf. I ask that their mind would be renewed and that you oh God would bless them more than they could have ever dreamed possible. Bind up this work that they have done and seal it. Create in them a clean heart and renew a right spirit within them. Anoint them to do what you have called them to do here on the earth. Infuse them with courage and strength. Provide them with people, resources, and opportunities to be a blessing to the brokenhearted. I pray that they will be deeply rooted in your love and able to stand firm when the winds of life blow hard. Help them to set their minds on things above and daily renew their strength. I commit them into your hands now and forevermore in Jesus' name. Amen!

FROM MY HEART TO YOURS:

Should you have hard days in the future that feel filled with grief and sorrow, please pause and grab a blanket, wrap yourself, and remember that God is right there with you! When you need a hand to hold, grab your gloves and remember that Christ is right there with you. Be mindful that the hard day will pass and that you are cherished by your Father in heaven. Allow yourself to feel the pain for a little while, but do not allow yourself to live in it. Strive to forget what lies behind as Paul said in Philippians 3:14. Strive to let go of the hurtful memories and pain. Shift your focus and think about things that are pure, lovely, and of good report. Look for the good on purpose. It's time to dream again, to get back to enjoying your gift of life! The time for walking around downcast, depressed, and lifeless in your spirit is now over! Pick up your head and move forward with your robe of righteousness and newfound strength as a whole and healed person.

If you now desire to send the letter you wrote out to the one(s) you hurt, please look back over it before you send it and make sure you have a peace in your soul before you do. When you have done these things and are at peace, go ahead and send your letter, but do so without any expectation from the other. Do it for yourself; what they decide to do with it is upon them.

I have been honored to travel with you on this journey. May your peace be great and your heart strong! If not before, I look forward to when we meet in heaven. Bless you dear one.

www.ingramcontent.com/pod-product-compliance
Lightning Source LLC
Chambersburg PA
CBHW062049090426

42740CB00016B/3066